Contents

KV-622-144

Table of Figures

AN INTRODUCTION TO SYSTEMIC GRAMMAR

by
G.D. MORLEY

Macmillan

Liverpool University
English Language Unit

First published 1985

Published by *Macmillan Publishers Ltd*
London and Basingstoke
*Associated companies and representatives in Accra,
Auckland, Delhi, Dublin, Gaborone, Hamburg, Harare,
Hong Kong, Kuala Lumpur, Lagos, Manzini, Melbourne,
Mexico City, Nairobi, New York, Singapore, Tokyo*

Printed in Hong Kong

British Library Cataloguing in Publication Data

Morley, G.D.
  An introduction to systemic grammar,
  1. Grammar, Comparative and general
  I. Title
  415   P151

ISBN 0-333-38261-7

Introduction

Systemic grammar was originally formulated by M.A.K. Halliday and can be traced through two principal stages of development. The early form of the theory was known as scale-and-category grammar (see Halliday:1961). Halliday had been a pupil of the British linguist J.R. Firth, and his formulation of scale-and-category theory owes much to the influence of Firth's teaching; it does, however, represent a substantial progression from Firth's own thinking. Scale-and-category grammar is set against the backcloth that language occurs in a situational context.
In common with transformational grammar attention in the first half of the 1960s was concentrated on syntax; but whereas transformational grammar is concerned with the generation of underlying, 'deep' structures and their subsequent transformation into well-formed surface structure sentences, scale-and-category grammar provides a framework for the analysis and description of any stretch of written or spoken language that has actually occurred.

During the latter half of the 1960s Halliday's work became increasingly influenced by ideas on the functional nature of language, as held for example by B. Malinowski, and a multifunctional semantic dimension was not merely added to systemic theory but became central to it (see Halliday:1967-8). With the inclusion of the semantic dimension, syntactic structure no longer held the same focus of attention, nor did the grammar seek just to analyse stretches of actual text. At the time of this reorientation the theory became known as systemic functional grammar, or systemic grammar for short. (Many linguists, indeed, now use the name 'systemic grammar' in referring to all work in the Hallidayan mould since 1961.) In its enhanced form the grammar began to account for the nature of the linguistic system available to the native speaker of a language and for the selection of options which a person makes when using the language. These options are selected not from the syntax but from the semantics of the grammar and thus represent the choices of meaning which the speaker/writer is expressing. The meaning options are then realised as component elements of the language structure, that is to say as the various contributory parts of the total lexical, syntactic and phonological structure of the language being spoken or written. Contemporary systemic grammar thus takes a completely opposite view of the role and place of semantics to any of the versions of the standard theory of transformational grammar; in systemic grammar semantics is the generative 'base', in transformational grammar it has a purely interpretative function.

This book is designed as a concise introductory survey of systemic theory with particular reference to the syntactic and semantic dimensions of the grammar. It is intended for undergraduate students of linguistics, postgraduate students of applied linguistics as well as for those in education concerned with language and language teaching. It is divided into two parts. Part 1 outlines the scale-and-category framework and the basic principles of systemic syntax. Part 2 then presents the reorientated multifunctional model and considers each of the components comprising the semantic dimension of the grammar. As already stated, the book is essentially an introductory survey. Few of the points made, therefore, are claimed to be original; most of the ideas are drawn from the writings of Halliday and other systemic grammarians, but responsibility is, of course, accepted for any infelicities of interpretation.

PART 1

SCALE-AND-CATEGORY GRAMMAR

1. Levels of Language

Scale-and-category grammar seeks to account for any stretch of language as it actually occurs, in either written or spoken form. It is thus not confined to analysing passages from books or other printed matter but handles equally the often more hesitant structures of conversation. By contrast with transformational grammar, however, scale-and-category is designed to analyse structures as they appear rather than to generate them. A stretch or corpus of language which is selected for description is referred to as 'text', irrespective of whether the material appears in the form of a printed script or oral recording. This early stage of systemic theory held that a text may be analysed at three primary levels: substance, form and situation.

1.1 Substance

Substance is the string of actual sounds that a person hears or the stretches of writing that a reader sees; more technically, substance denotes the phonic or graphic material to be studied. Variations in the way people with different regional accents might pronounce the same words or intonate the same utterance in the same context would exemplify variations of substance. The actual nature of sounds and their production, transmission and perception are studied under the science of phonetics; and by analogy the study of variations in people's handwriting may be termed graphetics.

1.2 Form

Form in scale-and-category theory is accounted for under two complementary sub-levels: grammar and lexis. Grammar is, broadly speaking, concerned with the nature of elements of structure and with the relationships which exist between them. It embraces the areas traditionally known as syntax — the grammar above the word — and morphology — the grammar below the word — and it is the principal focus of Part 1. Lexis, on the other hand, is concerned with the study of vocabulary (or, more precisely, lexical items) and with the regularities and patterns of co-occurrence which may be established between them. The term 'lexical item' is used in preference to word because, for example, many lexical items comprise more than a single word, e.g. *fire extinguisher, value added tax, driving licence.* It is also the case in scale-and-category theory that not all words are counted as lexical items: some words, e.g. *the, and, are, it,* are regarded as carrying grammatical rather than lexical meaning. Lexical studies in the early stages concentrated on establishing relationships of collocation, that it to say the co-occurrence of one lexical item with another. For example, *bread* may be observed in such collocations as *bread roll, bread knife, bread sauce, bread bin; bread and jam, bread and butter, bread and cheese, bread and water; cut the bread, slice the bread, butter the bread, jam the bread,* but not normally *bread fork, bread and cake, margarine the bread.* Lexical items which have roughly the same range of collocations are then grouped into lexical sets.

1.3 Situation

The study of situation is interpreted as lying outside the domain of linguistics. It involves an account of all the sociological factors which constitute the background to and circumstances of the text under discussion. This includes, for example, the location and time of the text, the previous events circumscribing it, the number of participants involved, the nature of their personalities, their status relationship in that particular situation, what they are talking about, and any accompanying actions or gestures.

1.4 Phonology

Linking the three levels of substance, form and situation are two interlevels: phonology/graphology and context. Phonology and graphology make up the interlevel between substance and form, and context the interlevel between form and situation. Phonology deals with the nature and patterning of units of sound in a particular language, and thus the value that the units have in that language. For the description of English, four phonological units are recognised: the phoneme, the syllable, the foot and the tone group.

Phonemes denote the individual sound units of a language; for example, the word *freeze* consists of four phonemes |friz|. Syllables mark the patterns of relative sound prominence in phoneme sequences, each syllable having one peak of prominence; thus |friz| is one syllable, whereas |semi| has two. Feet mark the stress patterns in syllable sequences, each foot having one strong stress, e.g. <u>yesterday</u>. Tone groups carry the intonation patterns, the description of which includes reference to the height and degree of movement of pitch contours within utterances. The essential difference between phonetics and phonology is that phonetics is concerned with the intrinsic nature of sounds, irrespective of the language or dialect being spoken, whereas phonology is interested in the value that the sounds have in the linguistic system of a particular language or dialect. Thus the front and dark l–sounds in *lip* and *pill* in standard English are phonetically different (alveolar and alveolar velarised respectively), but phonologically they are merely variants of the same phoneme. On the other hand, the hard and soft l–sounds in the Russian words *ugol* (corner) and *ugol'* (coal) are not just phonetically different (only the second is palatalised) but also phonologically distinct as they represent separate phonemes.

Graphology is the study of the writing systems employed by different languages. Among its concerns is, for example, the fact that English, Russian and Greek employ different alphabets — the Roman, Cyrillic and Greek — in each of which there is a fairly consistent correspondence between the pronunciation and spelling of words. By contrast, Chinese uses a logographic system of characters, in which each character represents a different word or morpheme, and Japanese combines the use of a logographic system with a syllabary, in which each symbol has a broadly syllabic value.

1.5 Context and register

The interlevel between form and situation is termed, as mentioned earlier, 'context'. Context serves to itemise those aspects of the situation which have a bearing on the form used. Work on context throughout the development of systemic theory has been undertaken under the heading of 'register'. Early studies of register were guided by the maxims that language varies with situation and that a certain kind of language is appropriate to a certain use. For example, the language of a legal document would not be that used in a doctor's surgery or at a dinner party. Thus register may be defined as the variety of a language used in a particular situational context.

To account for the aspects of situational context, four parameters are established at this stage: the field, the mode, the tenor and the role of the discourse. The field of discourse relates to the subject matter of the text — to what the text is about, e.g. mountaineering, choral music, gardening, neurophysiology, car maintenance, football. Mode specifies the medium of the text. The two basic modes are spoken (e.g. monologue, conversation) and written (e.g. reference book, newspaper article), but there are others involving both speech and writing: for example, written to be spoken (e.g. news bulletin), written as if spoken (e.g. dialogue in novel), spoken from written (e.g. reading story to child) and speaking what is written to be spoken as if not written (e.g. a play). These and other types of mode are shown in Figure 1.

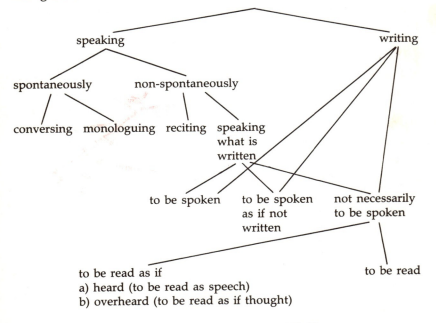

Fig. 1   Types of mode in register (Gregory and Carroll: 1978:47)

Tenor denotes the degree of formality and familiarity of the discourse. M. Joos (1962) proposed a five-term scale for this parameter:

frozen: *Miss Jones must keep silent.*
formal: *Kindly keep quiet, Miss Jones.*
consultative: *Miss Jones, would you mind not talking, please.*
casual: *Better not talk now, Mary.*
intimate: *Shsh, darling.*

To this list may be added further terms, e.g. informal, familiar, impersonal, colloquial, technical, etc. The degree of formality in turn reflects the status relationship of the participants in the situation in question, for example, manager-employee, doctor-patient, salesman-customer, judge-jury, plumber-householder, parent-child... Finally, the role of the discourse is its social function. Thus, *Could you pass the salt, please?* is a request, *Have a break, have a KitKat* is an advertisement, *If you do that again, I'll smack you* is a threat. Other roles include greeting, description, advice, direction, invitation, warning, joke, etc. Register varieties are thus obtained by matching particular groupings of situational features with the accompanying linguistic features: phonological, grammatical and lexical.

Scale-and-category theory thus sees linguistics as embracing the level of form, comprising grammar and lexis, together with the interlevels of phonology and context. The levels of substance and situation, constituting the phonetic expression of and the sociological background to the text, are not regarded as part of the linguistic system. (Semantics as such was not represented as a level in its own right in the early stages.) The relationship between the various levels and interlevels in scale-and-category theory is shown in Figure 2.

Substance	⟷	Form	⟷	Situation
phonetics	phonology	grammar lexis	context	sociological setting
		LINGUISTICS		

Fig. 2 Levels of language in scale-and-category theory

2. Categories and Scales

As explained in Section 1.2, grammatical form in scale-and-category theory is concerned with the nature of elements of structure and the relationships which may be established between them. To facilitate the determination of these elements and relationships, the grammar postulates four theoretical categories: unit, structure, class and system, and three (or four) scales: rank, exponence, delicacy (and depth).

2.1 Unit

The first category, unit, accounts for stretches of language of varying lengths and composition which themselves carry grammatical patterns or which operate in grammatical patterns. In the early stages of the theory five sizes of grammatical unit were proposed for the description of English: sentence, clause, group, word and morpheme. (As outlined in Section 4, however, some writers later replaced the term 'sentence' as a grammatical unit with the term 'clause complex'.) These may be illustrated as follows.

sentence
|||*When the climbers had reached the summit, they danced a reel.*|||

clause
|||*When the climbers had reached the summit,*|| *they danced a reel.*|||

group
|||*When*|*the climbers*|*had reached*|*the summit,*||*they*|*danced*|*a reel.*|||

word
|||*When*|*the*|*climbers*|*had*|*reached*|*the*|*summit,*||*they*|*danced*|*a*|*reel.*|||

morpheme
|||*When*|*the*|*climb*|*er*|*s*|*ha*|*d*|*reach*|*ed*|*the*|*summit,*||*they*|*dance*|*d*|*a*|*reel.*|||

Thus, although *climbers had* and *danced a* are stretches of language, they do not as pairs of words constitute group units in the way that *had reached* or *a reel* do.

As implied by the above presentation, scale-and-category

grammar regards the sentence as the largest grammatical unit and the morpheme as the smallest. The sentence is the largest unit carrying grammatical patterns, whereas the morpheme is the smallest unit entering into grammatical patterns. Thereafter, as will be explained later, each of the units is defined in terms of its relationship with other units rather than by reference to outside criteria.

The theory is aware of the importance of the coherence of content and the devices of cohesion which link sentences in the formation of larger stretches of text. Consider, for example, the following short passage.

Before setting off, make sure that you are properly equipped. For all mountain excursions boots are essential; without them your chances of slipping, getting wet feet or twisting an ankle are greatly increased. Similarly a waterproof and extra sweater should always be carried; the temperature at 3000' will be noticeably cooler than it was down in the valley.

The sentences comprising this small text do not exist in isolation from one another. Instead they form a unified whole throughout which the topic of mountaineering equipment is developed. The first sentence makes a general statement about the need for proper equipment; the second and third then detail specific items of equipment. Note the link between *for all mountain excursions* and *the temperature at 3000'* as also the relationship between *are essential* and *similarly*. An appreciation of the logicality of the content presentation and of the use of the cohesive links can be gained by now reading the sentences in the reverse order. All this does not, however, mean that scale-and-category theory regards the 'paragraph' as a larger grammatical unit.

2.2 Rank

The grammatical units are related to each other hierarchically through the scale of rank, as illustrated in Figure 3.

In accordance with this scale the units are arranged from the largest, the sentence, down to the smallest, the morpheme. Each unit except the largest is defined by its function in the structure of the unit next above, and conversely each unit except the smallest is composed of one or more units of the rank below. So a word, e.g. *climbers, reached, the,* consists of one or more

8

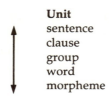

Unit
sentence
clause
group
word
morpheme

Fig. 3   Rank Scale

morphemes, viz. *climb|er|s, reach|ed, the.* A unit of group rank,
e.g. *they, have been painted, the climbers, the first ripe tomatoes from
the garden,* consists of one or more words. A clause consists of
one or more groups, e.g. *When|the climbers|had reached|the summit;
Jill|is playing|with her dolls; She|is reading; John!,* etc.

The grammar requires that all utterances be described in terms
of units at each rank. Thus, for example, *Jill is playing with her
dolls* is analysed as a sentence consisting of a clause containing
three groups comprising six words and eight morphemes. But it
also means that a reply *No* or *Three* is regarded as a sentence
consisting of one clause containing one group composed of one
word that is a single morpheme.

2.3   Structure

The second category, structure, accounts for the composition of a
unit in terms of functional elements and for the relationships
between these elements. For the description of English sentence
structure, two basic elements are recognised: free/alpha and
bound/beta. The value of these terms is essentially equivalent to
main and subordinate clauses in traditional terminology: main
clauses are classified as free/alpha, e.g. <u>John has lost his watch</u>,
<u>John said</u> that he had lost his watch; and adverbial, reported and
non-defining relative subordinate clauses as bound/beta,
e.g. <u>If you don't hurry</u>, you'll miss the train; I adore chocolate,
<u>which is an expensive pleasure</u>; John said <u>that he had lost his watch</u>.
However, whereas the traditional terms 'main' and 'subordinate'
and the scale-and-category labels 'alpha' and 'beta' are applied
according to their pivot and dependency functions within a
sentence, the term 'free' is subject to different constraints. An
element of sentence structure which is free ought to be capable

9

of functioning as a simple unit of sentence rank. *John has lost his watch, You'll miss the train* and *I adore chocolate* fulfil this requirement, but *John said* does not. In order to function as a sentence unit *John said* needs a completive element, which in the case of reported speech takes the form of what is traditionally termed a noun clause object. *John said* is thus alpha but not free. Omitted from the discussion here, defining relative clauses and many other types of noun clause are not analysed as bound/beta elements; treatment of them is considered later under 'rankshift' (Section 3.2).

The description of clause structure makes use of five elements, four of which are deemed primary: subject (S), predicator (P), complement (C) and adjunct (A), and one secondary: the Z-element. The subject is associated with the nominal group, the complement with the nominal or adjectival group, the predicator with the verbal group, and the adjunct with the adverbial group and the prepositional group.

Example:

> S   P   C   A   A
>
> *Susan|supped|her soup|silently|in the sun-lounge.*

Z is the label assigned to a nominal group which for one of several possible reasons is indeterminate as to subject or complement status. It may occur in titles, e.g. *A Tale of Two Cities, BBC Radio News, Moonlight Sonata,* or in vocative expressions, e.g. *The child ran off screaming, 'Mummy, Mummy!'* Z is also used in a sentence where the nominal group serves the functions of complement and subject simultaneously, e.g. *Jim helped his wife to wash up; Jack persuaded Fiona to come.* Thus in the first example *his wife* is both the complement of *helped* and the subject of *to wash up.* As will be appreciated, the rationale behind these types of Z-element is very different. With titles and vocatives the indeterminacy stems from the absence of a predicator, but in the third type it arises from a fusion of two functions.

An alternative way of representing the third type of Z-element is to mark discretely the two functions which are fused; this, indeed, is the method adopted by Young (1980:138-9), thus:

> S   P   C/S   P
>
> *Jim|helped|his wife|to wash up.*

```
    S       P      C/S     P
Jack|persuaded|Fiona|to come.

S    P    C/S    P         C
I|taught|him|to play|the piano.
```

Breaking the analysis down in this way in fact allows a distinction to be made between nominal elements whose indeterminacy is due to the absence of a predicator and those where it involves a fusion of functions. It also helps to differentiate the genuine double-function nominals in the three examples above from medial nominal elements which on the surface may seem the same but which in reality are not.

Examples:

Jack wanted Fiona to come.
Bill expected Susan to win.
Andrew liked Linda to drive.

In the first sentence here, what Jack wanted was not Fiona herself but that Fiona should come. In other words, *Fiona* is the subject of the infinitive *to come* but not by itself the complement of the verb *wanted:* the actual complement of this verb is the whole string *Fiona to come.* The same argument applies to the other two sentences.

The grammatical functions of *Fiona* in relation to the main verb *wanted* in a) *Jack wanted Fiona to come* and b) *Jack wanted Fiona* are thus quite separate. But the grammatical roles that *Fiona* fulfils in relation to the verb *persuaded* in a) *Jack persuaded Fiona to come* and b) *Jack persuaded Fiona* are the same. The nature of the contrast between the sentences *John wanted Fiona to come* and *Jack persuaded Fiona to come* is well illustrated by the following diagrams, based on but amended from Young (1980).

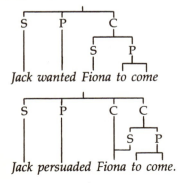

Jack wanted Fiona to come

Jack persuaded Fiona to come.

The structure of group rank units depends on the type or class of unit. The general nature of group structure may, however, be illustrated in a preliminary way using the terms modifier (m), head (h) and qualifier (q). The head element is the main or focal element of the group on which all other elements in the group depend syntactically. Elements of the group which precede the head may then be classed as modifiers and those which follow the head as qualifiers. Modifiers and qualifiers are thus identified by position in relation to the headword. These three terms can be applied most readily to the analysis of nominal, adjectival and adverbial groups.

Examples:

nominal: m   m   h
three blind mice

               m   h   q
the president elect

               m   m   m   h   q
his most amazing feat of endurance

               m   h   q
the achievement that John treasures most

adjectival: m   h   q
very warm indeed

               m   h
quite amazing

               h   q
happy enough

adverbial: m   h   q
very quickly indeed

               m   h
quite amazingly

               h   q
happily enough

In the nominal groups the qualifier elements may consist of a single word, as in *the president elect,* or a prepositional group, e.g. *his most amazing feat of endurance,* or even a defining relative clause, e.g. *the achievement that John treasures most.* The terms 'modifier', 'head' and 'qualifier' are less satisfactory for describing verbal and prepositional groups, the structure of which will therefore be left until the whole area is discussed in more detail under 'delicacy' (Section 2.7).

Word structure will not be pursued in any detail here, but its elementary nature may be illustrated with reference to the terms 'base' and 'affix'.

Examples:

base aff
reach|ed

aff base
en | rich

aff base aff aff
out|stand|ing| ly

It is worth noting that the term 'base' here does not imply that the element is free. Although the base in each of the instances above is free, it may in other examples be bound, e.g. *con<u>cord</u>, ex<u>hale</u>, ad<u>here</u>*.

2.4 Class

Members of a unit are grouped and assigned to a particular class firstly according to their similarities and differences of structure, secondly according to their function in the next largest unit, and thirdly according to how they combine with other units of the same rank. Since, in scale-and-category grammar, sentences do not operate in a larger grammatical unit, the second criterion does not apply to them. In terms of their formal structure, however, sentences are traditionally classified as simple, complex or compound. A simple sentence consists of a single free clause, e.g. *Bill has emigrated to America; When did he leave?* A complex sentence comprises a free clause together with one or more bound clauses, e.g. *When the king finally arrived, the royal banquet was begun.* A compound sentence is composed of two or more free clauses, e.g. *Jack fell down and broke his crown and Jill came tumbling after.* These three terms alone, however, do not satisfactorily handle sentences which are compound and yet contain one or more bound clauses, e.g. *If you get there before I do, just dig a hole and pull me through.* To cope with this type of structure a further term 'compound-complex' may be added.

Sentences are also traditionally classified according to their contextual function, using the basic labels 'statement', 'question', 'command/request' and 'exclamation'. (Clearly, utterances fulfil a much more detailed range of role functions than these, e.g. to urge, advise, insist, permit, etc., but within scale-and-category grammar the social role of an utterance is handled as a parameter of register.) Statements serve to convey information, e.g. *Susan has arrived; This is the eight o'clock news.* Questions elicit information, e.g. *Has Susan arrived yet?; When did she come?* Commands and requests are intended to control the behaviour of others and to get things done, e.g. *On your marks, get set, go!; Do not lean out of the window; Day return to Edinburgh, please.* Finally, exclamations give expression to feelings, e.g. *Good gracious!; Give me strength!; Heavens above!* These contextual classes are usually associated with a particular mood-patterning of the main clause: statement with declarative mood, question with interrogative, command with imperative, and exclamation with minor exclamative (moodless) utterances. But there is no automatic correlation. Thus, for example, the sentence *Susan has arrived?* has the declarative form associated with a statement but, given the appropriate intonation, it fulfils the contextual function of a question. Similarly *Will you tell Johnny to come home?* has the interrogative patterning of a question but the contextual function of a request. *New recruits will report for briefing at 10.00 a.m.* has the appearance of a statement but functions as a command. *Give me strength!* has the form of a command but operates as an exclamation.

At clause rank a distinction has already been drawn between free and bound classes of clause. The point was made that free clauses should potentially be able to operate as simple sentences, whereas bound clauses may not, as illustrated by the following examples.

bound	free
When the meeting had finished, || *we went for a meal.*	

free	bound
Yesterday we climbed Ben Lomond, || *which is a very popular walk.*	

According to whether they contain a predicator or not, free clauses are assigned to the classes major or minor.

Examples:

major: *I adore fresh strawberries.*
        Will you have cream with your strawberries?
minor: *Fresh strawberries for sale.*
        Not today, thank you.

In terms of their formal patterning, free clauses which have a predicator are assigned to a class of mood. Clauses containing a subject element are labelled indicative, and within this class two principal sub-types are recognised: declarative and interrogative. The term 'declarative' is applied to clauses with the sequence: subject + predicator, e.g. *The concert has begun; The chairman proposed a toast.* 'Interrogative' is the name given to clauses which contain one of a limited set of interrogative words, e.g. *who, what, why, when, where, how, which,* or which have an inverted word order in which frequently the verbal group is split and surrounds the subject, e.g. *Did Frank meet him?; Would you like some coffee?; Are you enjoying the course?; Have you had a reply yet?* Imperative clauses most commonly either omit the subject altogether or make use of an exhortative auxiliary, e.g. *Go home; Get out; Let's go home; Let's get out of here.*

Earlier in this section an outline was given of how sentences are traditionally classified according to their contextual function. However, this classification should really apply not to the sentence as a whole but rather to each of the constituent free clauses or clause complexes centring round a free clause. The point is brought out by the analysis of certain compound sentences e.g. *Will you make the tea please and I'll get the milk out; Get upstairs at once or I'll smack you.* These sentences comprise two free clauses, each of which performs a different contextual function. In the first example these are a request and a statement, in the second a command and a statement. To try to assign just one contextual role to either sentence purely because it is bounded by a capital letter and a full stop would be inappropriate. The classification of utterances in terms of their contextual function may thus be transferred from the sentence to the free clause.

Within bound clauses scale-and-category grammar has recognised three functional classes: conditioning (or contingent), additioning (or adding), and reported. Conditioning bound clauses serve to modify the information in the clause to which they are subordinated by placing a constraint or 'condition' on the content of the superordinate clause, e.g. *If at first you don't succeed, try, try and try again; Let me know, when you get a reply; Before John left, he watered the plants; Jean missed the train because she got up too late.* An additioning clause supplies further, optional information in the form of an aside or a comment on all or a part of the content of the superordinate clause, e.g. *As you know, linguistics has mushroomed since the 1950s; I adore chocolate, which is very bad for me; Ian, who is now twenty-six, is getting married next month.* Reported clauses include reported speech, e.g. *The student said that he preferred syntax; The reporter enquired where the animal had been caught; The child wondered if the rain would ever stop.*

Units of group rank were first classified as nominal, verbal and adverbial. More recently, adjectival and prepositional groups have been added as classes in their own right, distinct from the nominal and adverbial groups (see especially Fawcett: 1974-6/1981). It is therefore now possible to define a group according to the nature of the head element. Thus a nominal group normally has a noun as headword, an adjectival group an adjective as headword, etc.

Examples:

nominal verbal adjectival
Jill | was | very happy.

nominal verbal adverbial
This new model | has sold | very quickly indeed.

nom adv vbl nominal prepositional
You | always | get | a warm welcome | in Scotland.

Nominal groups usually operate in the structure of the subject, complement or Z-element. Adjectival groups function as complements, verbal groups as predicators, and adverbial and prepositional groups are principally associated with adjuncts.

2.5 System

The fourth category, system, accounts for the range of choices (classes) which are available within a unit, and any given range of possible options is known as a set of 'terms'. Thus, for example, the relations between the terms from the system of mood, outlined in the previous section on 'class', may be set out as follows.

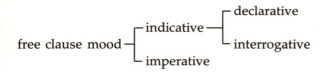

free clause mood — indicative — declarative / interrogative; imperative

Two important properties of a system are that the list of terms contained in it is finite and that the options are all mutually exclusive, so that if a new term is added the meaning of at least one of the existing terms is affected. As a crude analogy, a system accounting for a particular area of grammar may be likened to the number of pieces into which a cake is cut; the size of the cake remains constant, but the size of each slice depends on the number of portions into which the cake is divided. So, for example, we could not add a further choice option to indicative and imperative without affecting the scope and nature of one or both of these terms. This is not to say, however, that we cannot develop a system through the establishment of sub-systems. We have already shown that the term indicative in the initial system opens up a further system with the choice between declarative and interrogative. But these further options do not change the form of the initial system, rather the prior selection of 'indicative' serves as an entry condition to this sub-system. Examples of other systems discussed so far are shown with slight modifications in the diagrams below.

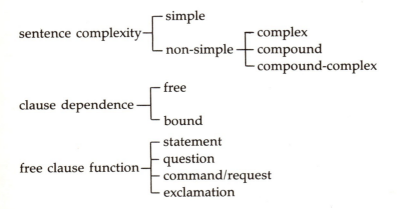

sentence complexity — simple / non-simple — complex / compound / compound-complex

clause dependence — free / bound

free clause function — statement / question / command/request / exclamation

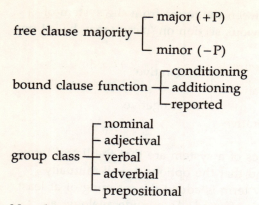

free clause majority ┬ major (+P)
                     └ minor (−P)

bound clause function ┬ conditioning
                      ├ additioning
                      └ reported

group class ┬ nominal
            ├ adjectival
            ├ verbal
            ├ adverbial
            └ prepositional

Now here are some of the systems which can be applied to verbal groups:

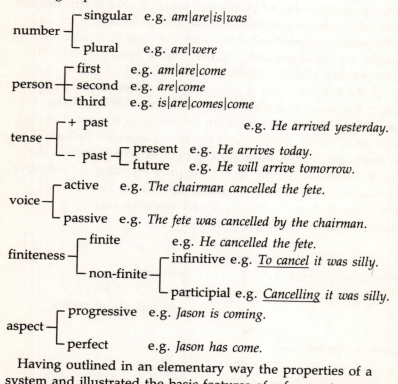

number ┬ singular e.g. *am|are|is|was*
       └ plural   e.g. *are|were*

person ┬ first   e.g. *am|are|come*
       ├ second e.g. *are|come*
       └ third   e.g. *is|are|comes|come*

tense ┬ + past   e.g. *He arrived yesterday.*
      └ − past ┬ present e.g. *He arrives today.*
               └ future   e.g. *He will arrive tomorrow.*

voice ┬ active   e.g. *The chairman cancelled the fete.*
      └ passive e.g. *The fete was cancelled by the chairman.*

finiteness ┬ finite   e.g. *He cancelled the fete.*
           └ non-finite ┬ infinitive e.g. *To cancel* it was silly.
                        └ participial e.g. *Cancelling* it was silly.

aspect ┬ progressive e.g. *Jason is coming.*
       └ perfect   e.g. *Jason has come.*

Having outlined in an elementary way the properties of a system and illustrated the basic features of a few systems at different ranks, we now return to the rank of clause, in order firstly to develop in more detail the system of mood, and secondly to introduce a further system, transitivity, and with it

18

the domain of complementation. These two systems, mood and transitivity, have been given greater emphasis in later models of systemic grammar.

The system shown in Figure 4, adapted from Huddleston's exposition (1981), extends the earlier system of mood in the free clause.

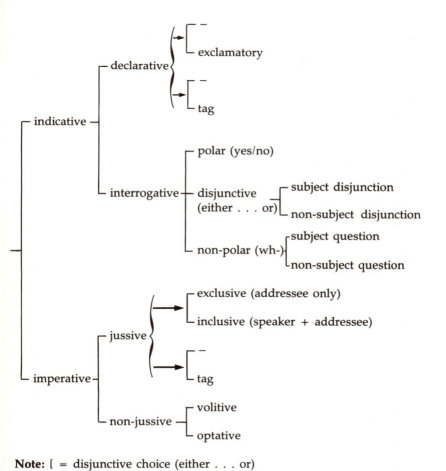

Note: [= disjunctive choice (either . . . or)
    { = simultaneous choice (both . . . and)

Fig. 4 System of mood

Examples:

INDICATIVE

declarative: *John saw Peter.*

declarative, exclamatory: *What a lot of people saw Peter!*

declarative, tag: *John saw Peter, didn't he?*

declarative, exclamatory, tag: *What a lot of people saw Peter, didn't they?*

interrogative, polar: *Did John see Peter?*

interrogative, disjunctive, subject disjunctive: *Did John or Mary see Peter?*

interrogative, disjunctive, non-subject disjunctive: *Did John see Peter or Jill?*

interrogative, non-polar, subject question: *Who saw Peter?*

interrogative, non-polar, non-subject question: *What did Peter see?*

IMPERATIVE

jussive, exclusive: *Shut up!*

jussive, inclusive: *Let's go.*

jussive, exclusive, tag: *Shut up, will you?*

jussive, inclusive, tag: *Let's go, shall we?*

non-jussive, volitive: *May you be forgiven.*

non-jussive, optative: *Let ABC be an equilateral triangle.*

The system of transitivity in the clause is concerned with the nature of complementation, that is to say with the way in which the predicator combines with different types of complement. In order to appreciate the organisation of this system it is necessary to understand something of the various types of complement element which occur. The complement element in clause structure may be subdivided into extensive (C^e) and intensive (C^i) complements. An extensive complement, with the exception of reflexive forms, is a nominal entity which is distinct from the subject; it thus corresponds to the traditional grammatical notion of object.

Examples:

John visited the doctor.
Bill has a new job.
The manager gave me a gold watch.

An intensive complement, on the other hand, is an entity or feature which is co-referential with the subject and which indeed in traditional grammar would also be referred to as a complement.

Examples:

> Tony is <u>the chairman</u>.
> Jane is <u>a doctor</u>.
> Jane is <u>a good doctor</u>.
> Jim is <u>ill.</u>

Within extensive complements a distinction is normally drawn between elements traditionally referred to as direct objects (C^{e1}) and indirect objects (C^{e2}).

Examples:

$$\quad\quad\quad C^{e2} \quad\quad C^{e1}$$
Sally|passed|me|the jam.

$$\quad\quad\quad\quad C^{e2} \quad\quad\quad C^{e1}$$
The manager|gave|me|a gold watch.

It should be noted, however, that where the recipient is expounded by a prepositional group, scale-and-category grammar has analysed it an an adjunct. Intensive complements function either attributively or equatively: attributively they may denote a feature or membership of a class which is ascribed to the subject; equatively they may signify an entity which is identifiable with the subject, or even one identifiable *as* the subject.

Examples:

$$\quad\quad\quad C^{i\ att}$$
Jane|is|a doctor.

$$\quad\quad\quad\quad C^{i\ att}$$
Jane|is|a good doctor.

$$\quad\quad C^{i\ att}$$
Jim|is|ill.

$$\quad\quad\quad C^{i\ equ}$$
Tony|is|the chairman.

$$\quad\quad\quad\quad C^{i\ equ}$$
The chairman|is|Tony.

Lastly, intensive complements may be marked according to whether they co-refer to the subject (C^{is}) or to the complement (C^{ic}).

Examples:

$$C^{is}$$
Tony|is|the chairman.

$$C^{is}$$
Jane|is|a doctor.

$$C^{is}$$
Jim|is|ill.

$$C^{ic}$$
They|elected|Tony|chairman.

$$C^{ic}$$
Mary|made|Angus|a happy man.

$$C^{ic}$$
Mary|made|Jim|ill.

$$C^{is}$$
Nina|made|John|a good wife.

This information on complementation may be used to map out a system of transitivity of the clause (see Figure 5).

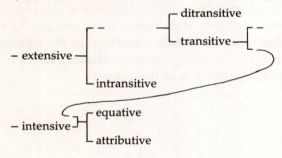

Fig. 5   System of transitivity in syntax

Key:

extensive = + lexical verb, e.g. *have, acquire, give,* many of which take an extensive complement.

intensive = + copular verb, e.g. *be, seem, become,* together with obligatory intensive complement.

intransitive = – extensive complement.

transitive = + extensive complement, C^{e1}.

ditransitive = + two extensive complements, C^{e1} and C^{e2}.

Examples:

extensive, ditransitive: *John gave Mary a necklace.*
                                        She passed me the salt.

extensive, transitive: *Mary has a new typewriter.*
                                          Bill broke the window.

extensive, intransitive: *He fell.*
                                          The children slept soundly.

intensive, equative: *Tony is the chairman.*
                                          The leader is John.

intensive, attributive: *Jim is ill.*
                                          Jack is a pilot.
                                          Jack is a good pilot.
                                          She made him a good wife.

extensive, transitive, equative: *They made him leader.*

extensive, transitive, attributive: *They made him ill.*

It should be finally pointed out that it is from the category of system, with its greatly increased importance, that the name 'systemic grammar' is derived.

2.6 Exponence

The scale of exponence is described as relating the categories to each other and to the data. By proceeding down this scale, changing rank as necessary, the description accounts grammatically and then lexically for the formal nature of a unit utterance. This process of grammatical description involves relating the functional structure of a unit to its formal exponents. In terms of this scale, the structure of a sentence consists of a number of elements denoted by the Greek letters alpha and beta; each of these elements is expounded by a unit of clause rank (with a change of rank). The structure of a clause is described in terms of the elements S, P, C, A and Z (see Section 2.3), which are expounded by units of group rank (with a change of rank); at group rank the class of unit—nominal, adjectival, verbal, adverbial or prepositional—is normally stated. Each group has a structure, consisting for example of the elements m, h and q, which are expounded by units of word rank (with a change of rank); again the class of word is usually given. Having concluded the grammatical analysis, the description moves on to list the lexical exponents.

Example:

John likes peaches.

#S# → α
α ↘ clause
clause → SPCᵉ
S ↘ nom grp
nom grp → h
h ↘ word: proper noun
proper noun ↘ *John*
P ↘ vb grp
vb grp → h
h ↘ word: verb (3rd person, singular, present tense)
verb ↘ *likes*
Cᵉ ↘ nom grp
nom grp → h
h ↘ word: noun (plural)
noun ↘ *peaches*

Key: → = has the structure of
↘ = is expounded by

2.7 Delicacy

The scale of delicacy determines the degree of detail in the analysis. In contrast with the scale of exponence it is rank-bound and therefore does not involve changes of rank. Units of clause rank have already been classified at the primary degree of delicacy into free/alpha and bound/beta clauses. At the secondary degree of delicacy they may be analysed in terms of an extended system of Greek letters marking the degree of grammatical subordination or distance from the alpha clause: alpha (α), beta (β), gamma (γ), delta (δ), epsilon (ε), etc.

Example:

primary:	free	bound
secondary:	α	β

Bill said||that he couldn't go||

primary:	bound	bound
secondary:	γ	δ

if payment was required||before he got his salary.

Analysis at the secondary degree highlights the fact that the bound clauses do not stand in an equal relationship of subordination to the free clause but that there exists a dependency relationship between them as well. Furthermore, it is possible in different sentences for the same subordinate clauses to stand in a different dependency relationship to the alpha clause; this will, of course, reflect the differences in meaning between the sentences in question. Compare the above example with the two that follow.

$$\beta \qquad\qquad \alpha \qquad\qquad \beta$$

Before he got his salary||Bill said||that he couldn't go||

$$\gamma$$

if payment was required.

$$\beta \qquad\qquad \gamma \qquad\qquad \alpha$$

If payment was required||before he got his salary||Bill said||

$$\beta$$

that he couldn't go.

The different types of complement have already been outlined as a preliminary to the system of transitivity. A distinction was made first between extensive and intensive complements (C^e and C^i). Two types of extensive complement were described, corresponding to the traditional direct and indirect objects. Intensive complements were subdivided according to whether they function attributively or equatively and according to whether they are intensive to the subject or to an extensive complement. This more delicate system of complementation is shown in Figure 6.

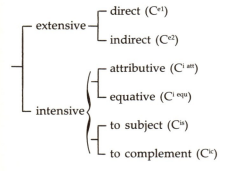

Fig. 6   System of complementation

Relatively little work has been done within a scale-and-category framework to disentangle the domain of the adjunct. A distinction is, however, made between adjuncts fulfilling linking or binding functions and those with a more lexical role. Linkers include co-ordinating conjunctions, e.g. *and, or, but*, and sentence adverbs providing a logical or commentative link, e.g. *however, therefore, nevertheless, consequently, yet, moreover, thus*, etc. Binders cover the class of words traditionally known as subordinating conjunctions, which bind clauses in a formal dependency relationship, e.g. *that, if, when, as, although, after, because, since, until, while*, etc. Lexical adjuncts are typically expounded in three ways: by the adverbial group, e.g. *The runners set off amazingly fast; We greatly admire your progress; Jack drives very carefully*; by a prepositional group, e.g. *In the summer John goes to Spain; After dinner he likes to sit in the garden*; and by the nominal group alone, e.g. *The next time Gerry was more cautious; The order arrived this morning*. Quirk et al. (1972) enumerate a wide range of meanings encompassed by adjuncts, as illustrated briefly below:

viewpoint: e.g. *politically, geographically, technically*.

focusing: e.g. *precisely, mainly, similarly, as well*.

intensifier: e.g. *obviously, totally, quite, at all*.

process: e.g. *thoroughly, by car, with a bullet*.

subject: e.g. *resentfully, with great pride, deliberately*.

formulaic: e.g. *kindly, please, cordially*.

place: e.g. *above, nearby, here, somewhere*.

time: e.g. *today, always, every week, already*.

reason: e.g. *because of* (prepositional group), *since* (clause).

In Section 2.3 the structure of the nominal group was described in terms of modifier, head and qualifier. At the secondary degree of analysis the class of deictics (or determiners) may be distinguished from other modifiers; these include words such as articles, e.g. *a, the*, demonstratives, e.g. *this, that*, possessives, e.g. *my, your, his, our, their*, and quantifiers, e.g. *all (of), some, several, both*. At a still greater degree of delicacy, further terms have been introduced to give the following range: deictic (d), ordinal (o) covering numerals, epithet (e) denoting adjectives, nominal (n) denoting a modifying noun, head (h) and qualifier (q). The three degrees of delicacy outlined are illustrated on the next page.

	the|first|real|union|bid|for power					
primary:	m	m	m	m	h	q
secondary:	d	m	m	m	h	q
tertiary:	d	o	e	n	h	q

This tertiary degree is not, however, applied to analyses in this book.

Adverbial group structure has so far been described in terms of modifier (m), head (h) and qualifier (q), e.g. *very slowly indeed, quite quickly enough*. The alternative terms 'temperer' (t), 'apex' (a) and 'limiter' (l), respectively, are also found in the literature for these roles.

In recognising the adjectival group as discrete from the nominal group, Fawcett (1974-6/1981) also draws attention to the commonality of structure between adverbial and adjectival groups.

Compare:

He\|acted\|very quickly indeed.
His action\|was\|very quick indeed.

Although each has its own distinctive function, both groups are analysable in terms of the same elements: modifier, head and qualifier (or temperer, apex and limiter).

To describe the composition of the prepositional group the labels 'preposition' (p) and 'completive' (c) may be used as the basic elements.

Example:

             p   c
Susan\|is sitting\|in the lounge

Sometimes the preposition is preceded by an element modifying or intensifying the force of the preposition, e.g. *very near the fire, almost at the window, just over the hedge*. For this function the labels 'modifier' (m) or 'temperer' (t) may be found. Analysis of the sub-structure of the completive must then be given. Where this is a nominal group, its elements will be determiner, modifier, head and qualifier.

Examples:

p   c
    h
in Scotland

```
      p        c
    d   m   h     q
```
from the next president elect

```
  p      c
d   h      q
```
to the end of the road

Berry regards prepositional completives which consist of more than one word, that is to say of a group or clause, as rankshifted (see Section 3.2), and she then analyses their constituent structure accordingly. Sinclair (1972:148), on the other hand, views the prepositional group as a compounding of an adverbial and a nominal group without either of them being rankshifted. The approach here follows Sinclair's position in avoiding rankshift where the completive is expounded by a unit of group rank. It does, of course, sometimes happen that the completive is expounded by a clause unit, e.g. *by completing the crossword, from being a good employee, without taking a trick,* in which case rankshift is acknowledged.

For the description of the verbal group, the terms 'auxiliary' (a), 'head' (h) and 'particle' (p) may be used.

Examples:

```
    a    h    p
```
John|has given up.

```
    a   a    h
```
Bill|may be coming.

The head is the main verb, while the term 'auxiliary' refers to any auxiliary verb. The verbs *to be, to do* and *to have* can thus operate as either headwords or auxiliaries.

Examples:

```
    h
```
She|is|ill.

```
    h
```
You|did|very well.

```
    h
```
Jill|has|a cold.

```
    a   h
```
Jack|is going|to Spain.

```
     a   h
Jack|did go|to Spain.

     a   h
Jack|has gone|to Spain.
```

In place of 'head' the terms 'verb' (v) and 'lexical element' (l) are also to be found. But 'lexical element' would not be suitable for specifying the main verb in a sentence such as *Bob is away:* although *is* in this sentence is the head of the verbal group, it is regarded as a grammatical rather than a lexical verb.

2.8 Depth

The scale of depth is not always handled separately from the scale of delicacy, but it does in fact fulfil a quite distinct role. Whereas the scale of delicacy is concerned with the degree of detail of the analysis, the scale of depth considers the degree of complexity of a stretch of language. The depth of an element of structure is the relationship between that element and the top node or point of origin in the structure: the more nodes or stages by which the element is removed from the top node, the greater the depth of the element. Thus a delta clause represents a stage of greater depth in structure than a beta clause, as illustrated by Figure 7.

Fig. 7   Scale of depth

To show the distinction between delicacy and depth three types of contrast may be instanced. The difference between the analysis of nominal group structure, e.g. *the fortieth American president elect*, as either mmmhq or doehq is one of delicacy, or degree of detail, only; the elements doehq involve no increase in depth over mmmhq. The difference in the analysis of the three-clause sentence *Tell me if your leg still hurts when you take your weight off it* as free + bound + bound or as alpha + beta + gamma involves both delicacy and depth; the inclusion of 'gamma' gives more detail about the relationships of subordination between the component clauses, and 'gamma' also marks a node which is one place further removed in depth from the top node than 'bound' can ever be. However the difference in structure between the two-clause sentence *Bill said that he couldn't go*, analysed as alpha + beta, and the four-clause sentence *Bill said that he couldn't go if payment was required before he got his salary*, analysed as alpha + beta + gamma + delta, is a question of depth alone.

3. Complexity

3.1 Recursion

The nature and scope of the scale of depth needs to be understood within the more general concept of recursion. Recursion is the name given to structural relationships in which an element is repeated to form a progression. Structures involving recursion may be classified into two main types: linear and embedded. Linear recursion involves units of the same rank which are adjoined in a relationship of coordination and subordination.

Examples:

Jack fell down||and broke his crown||and Jill came tumbling after.

Ring me||if you get home||before Jill arrives.

Embedded recursion involves units which operate as though they were members of a lower rank.

Examples:

Playing the flute is not easy.
The end of the fence is broken.

Within linear recursion two sub-types are recognised: paratactic and hypotactic. Paratactic linear recursion involves elements of equal grammatical status (for example, all alpha elements) whose order may reflect a precedence or progression in reality. Many compound sentences exhibit paratactic linear recursion.

Examples:

α^a α^b α^c
John jumped out of bed,||hurriedly dressed,||ate his breakfast||
α^d
and rushed off to work.

α^a α^b α^c
Jack fell down||and broke his crown,||and Jill came tumbling after.

Here each of the components is an alpha clause, so in syntactic terms none is subordinate to another, but the sequence of the clauses is crucial as it reflects a contextual ordering. Thus, for example, John's rushing off to work follows his eating, which follows his dressing, which follows his jumping out of bed. Indeed, to reverse the order of these clauses would be counter to reality and make nonsense. Consequently, superscript letters may be used, as above, to mark this precedence. In a syntactically similar sentence the order of the elements may not imply any order in reality but merely serves to list the events or entities involved. In such a case no additional superscript marking is needed.

Examples:

$\overset{\alpha}{John}$ enjoys athletics,$||\overset{\alpha}{collects}$ stamps$||\overset{\alpha}{and}$ sings in the local choral society.

$We|\overset{\alpha}{saw}|a$ $\overset{\alpha}{lion}$, a $\overset{\alpha}{tiger}$, a $\overset{\alpha}{giraffe}$ and a hippo.

Further examples of paratactic linear recursion are to be found in relationships of apposition. To indicate the syntactic and referential equivalence a superscript stroke is inserted after each element.

Examples:

$\overset{\alpha'}{tomorrow}$, $\overset{\alpha'}{Friday}$, the $\overset{\alpha'}{fifteenth}$ of March

$\overset{\alpha'}{Bill}$, the $\overset{\alpha'}{baker}$

$\overset{\alpha'}{my}$ morning paper, the $\overset{\alpha'}{Daily}$ Guardian

Hypotactic linear recursion was illustrated when the scale of depth was first introduced. It involves the repetition of a type of element, forming a progression of grammatical dependence or a presupposition of occurrence.

Examples:

$\overset{\alpha}{John}$ explained$||\overset{\beta}{that}$ he couldn't come$||\overset{\gamma}{unless}$ Bill waited$||$

$\overset{\delta}{until}$ the meeting finished.

$\overset{\alpha}{Ring}$ me$||\overset{\beta}{if}$ you get home$||\overset{\gamma}{before}$ Jill arrives.

32

$$\overset{\alpha}{} \qquad\qquad \overset{\beta}{}$$

I love chocolate,||which is very bad for me.

$$\overset{\alpha}{} \quad \overset{\beta}{}$$

John|is|clever, if stupid.

3.2 Rankshift

Embedded recursion, which in scale-and-category grammar is known as rankshift, is where a recursive structure cuts across the scale of rank. Instead of operating in the structure of a unit of the next rank above, as is normally the case, the rankshifted unit enters into the structure of a unit of its own rank or even a unit of the rank below. A unit may thus be involved in single or double rankshift. There is single rankshift when a clause acts as a subject or complement in clause structure, e.g. *What you need is a decent piano; Playing the flute is not easy; Jane bought what she liked*, or where a unit of group rank functions as a qualifier in group structure, e.g. *The man over the road has a new car; We discussed John's objection to the proposal*. The principal type of double rankshift is found with restrictive relative clauses, where the subordinate clause operates as a qualifier in group structure, e.g. *This is the man who broke the record; The ticket that I was given is not valid*.

Rankshifted groups and clauses are marked by adding a short, inward-pointing, horizontal line to the top and bottom of each group division line or each pair of clause division lines. The full internal structure of each rankshifted element is then analysed, as demonstrated below with the foregoing examples.

```
          S          P     C^i equ
     C^el  S    P    h  d   m      h
     h    h    h
||| [What|you|need] |is|a decent piano.|||
```

```
     S    P              C^el
     h    h    C^el  S    P
               h    h    h
|||Jane|bought|[what |she|liked].|||
```

33

```
              S                    P      C^el
    d    h    q              h  d  m  h
              p         c
              d     h
|||The man [over the road] |has|a new car.|||
```

```
    S    P              C^el
    h    h         d    h    q
                        p         c
                        d         h
|||We|discussed|John's objection [to the proposal].|||
```

```
    S    P    C^i equ
    h    h    d    h    q
                    S    P      C^el
                    h    h    d    h
|||This|is|the man [who|broke|the record].|||
```

```
    S                          P  C^i att
    d    h    q              h neg  h
              C^el S      P
              h    h  a   h
|||The ticket [that|I|was given] |is|not valid.|||
```

The label 'neg' is an abbreviation for 'negative'.

3.3 Discontinuity

The sentences analysed so far have contained only whole clauses, one after another. In normal speech, however, it quite often happens that one element of sentence or clause structure is interrupted by another element; then after the intervention the structure of the original element is completed. An intervening clause is enclosed in double angle brackets, and an intervening group in single angle brackets.
Examples:

```
    α                    β
You'll find me <<if you want me>> in the library.
```

<pre>
        α   β   γ
</pre>
The athlete was told‖that <<because his entry form had not arrived>>
he could not run.

<pre>
        S   P   A   A
</pre>
The meeting|was <again> interrupted|by hecklers.

<pre>
   A   P   S   C
</pre>
How|did <you> manage|it?

The name given to this type of occurrence is discontinuity, and
the interrupted element is referred to as discontinuous.

3.4 Phase

A particular feature of scale-and-category grammar is its
traditional treatment of complex verbal sequences involving two
or more lexical elements, e.g. *He began to learn Chinese; He wanted*
to go home. The usual analysis of *began to learn* and *wanted to go*
has been to say that they each involve two verbal groups
expounding two predicators and that these two predicators
coexist in a relationship of phase within the framework of a
single clause. Examples of phase have then been marked by
linking the two predicators with a dotted line, as shown below.

<pre>
   S   P- - - - -P   C
</pre>
He|began to learn|Chinese.

<pre>
   S   P- - - -P   A
</pre>
He|wanted to go|home.

In the following further examples it will be seen also that an
adjectival complement or nominal element may appear between
the two predicators.

<pre>
   S P- - C- - - - -P   C
</pre>
He|is|eager|to read|this book.

<pre>
   S   P- - - - C - - -P
</pre>
He|seemed|happy|to stay.

<pre>
   S   P- - - - -P   C
</pre>
We|enjoyed reading|the book.

S P‑ ‑ ‑ ‑ ‑ ‑P C
I|hated reproaching|her.

S P‑ ‑ Z‑ ‑P C
Jack|persuaded|Jill|to learn|Chinese.

S P‑ ‑ ‑Z‑ ‑P C
Bob|helped|me|build|the house.

S P‑ ‑ ‑Z‑ ‑ ‑P C
Jack|wanted|Jill|to learn|Chinese.

S P‑ ‑ Z‑ ‑ ‑ ‑P C
I|hated|you|reproaching|her.

S P‑ ‑ ‑Z‑ ‑P Z‑ ‑ ‑ ‑P Z‑ ‑ ‑ ‑ ‑P
He|told|John|to ask|Sue|to invite|Frank|to come.

Arguments cited for the treatment of such verbal structures in this manner include the fact that phase is expounded by linear sequence such that the non-finite predicator cannot precede the finite predicator. There is also the point that phased elements normally occur within a single tone group. It is further argued that, by contrast with phased structures, bound conditioning clauses with a non-finite predicator can either precede or follow the superordinate clause, e.g. *Having worked at full stretch all day, John finally arrived home; John finally arrived home, having worked at full stretch all day; To buy a computer John has sold his car; John has sold his car to buy a computer.* In addition, bound clauses have their own tone group.

In spite of these arguments, however, the treatment of such structures in terms of phase glosses over their structural complexity. In the first place, the Z-element is used by grammarians adopting the phase analysis because it is considered that the medial nominal groups concerned act as complement and subject respectively to the preceding and following predicators. However, as was pointed out when Z-elements were discussed in Section 2.3, this reading of the situation does not apply to all such medial nominal elements. In many instances, for example *Jack wanted Jill to learn Chinese* and *I hated you reproaching her* above, the medial nominal is not by itself an extensive complement of the main, finite verb; it is, of course, the subject of the following non-finite verb construction and as a constituent of that non-finite construction does form part of the complex complement of the main, finite verb. Thus, whereas in *Jack persuaded Jill to learn Chinese* the nominal *Jill* does function both as complement of *persuade* and as subject of *to learn*, in the sentence *Jack wanted Jill to learn Chinese, Jill* is the subject of *to learn* but only part of the larger structure *Jill to learn Chinese*, which as a whole functions as the complement of *wanted*. Hence the assertion that the use of Z for all types of phase merely conceals a fundamental underlying distinction.

Secondly, linking the predicators involved in phase masks the relationship of syntactic presupposition which exists between them. In the sentences *Jack persuaded Jill to learn Chinese* and *Jack wanted Jill to learn Chinese* both occurrences of the non-finite verb *to learn* stand at a secondary degree of depth to the main verbs *persuaded* and *wanted*. In this respect, therefore, *persuaded* and *wanted* share common ground, and analysis of *to learn* needs to reflect its subordinate position to the appropriate superordinate, main verb. Furthermore, analysis of sentences with phased predicators should also be consistent with that of sentences having the same main, finite verb but which do not contain a secondary, non-finite verb.

Compare:

> *Jack wanted a new car.*
> *Jack wanted Jill.*
> *Jack wanted to learn Chinese.*
> *Jack wanted Jill to learn Chinese.*

The structure of *Jack wanted a new car* and *Jack wanted Jill* is straightforwardly $S+P+C$, *a new car* and *Jill* being the entities wanted. To achieve the desired consistency with the description of *Jack wanted to learn Chinese* and *Jack wanted Jill to learn Chinese*, and indeed for the description of all sentences containing interlocking predicators, the rankshift mechanism outlined earlier is advocated in place of a phase analysis. In the case of the two examples with the main verb *wanted* immediately above, this will record *to learn Chinese* and *Jill to learn Chinese* as rankshifted complements. As a result, the basic structure of all four examples above with the main verb *wanted* will be analysed as $S+P+C$.

```
    S    P          C
              P          C
Jack|wanted| [to learn|Chinese].
    S    P      C
              S    P        C
Jack|wanted|[Jill|to learn|Chinese].
```

It is, of course, to be appreciated that, in *Jack wanted to learn Chinese*, *Jack* is also the understood subject of the rankshifted element *to learn Chinese*. This could be recorded by a minor addition to the analysis.

```
    S    P              C
(S)            P          C
Jack|wanted| [to learn Chinese].
```

In the case of sentences with verbs like *persuaded* the situation is somewhat different.

Compare:

Jack persuaded Jill.

Jack persuaded Jill to learn Chinese.

In contrast with the argument that the sentence *Jack wanted Jill* does not form whole constituents of *Jack wanted Jill to learn Chinese*, the constituents of *Jack persuaded Jill* are whole constituents of *Jack persuaded Jill to learn Chinese*. In other words *Jill* is a discrete complement of *persuaded* in both instances. Using the mechanism of rankshift, however, we can determine two complements in the main clause of the sentence *Jack persuaded Jill to learn Chinese*.

```
    S      P      C         C
              (S)     P       C
Jack|persuaded|Jill| [to learn|Chinese].
```

Here the complement *Jill* of the predicator *persuaded* is also the understood subject of the rankshifted clause.

4. Modifications to the Framework

In Halliday's more recent writings, considerably less attention is paid to the individual categories and scales, and the changes which are made reflect a modified view of the level of form as a whole. To begin with, the phrase 'level of form' is replaced by the term 'lexico-grammatical stratum'. Under this revised heading are to be found significant alterations for the handling of formal structure.

Only four grammatical units are now recognised: clause, group, word and morpheme. The sentence has thus disappeared as a grammatical unit, and the term 'clause complex' is introduced to denote the largest grammatical structure. In fact the concept of a unit complex is introduced for units at each rank. Morphemes may combine to form a morpheme complex, words a word complex, groups a group complex, and clauses a clause complex. The nature of a unit complex, as it is usually interpreted, may be seen from the various illustrations below.

clause complex: *Jack fell down and Jill came tumbling after.*
Once Keith had got his degree, his confidence increased dramatically.
(nominal) group complex: *We bought a radio, a record player and a television.*
His first book, on singing technique, comes out next week.
(adjectival) word complex: *Mark has a very hit and miss approach.*
He is a good, though erratic, student.

The disappearance of the sentence as a grammatical unit can perhaps be explained by the increased interest in the nature and structure of text as distinct from grammatical structure alone. Clearly grammatical units are integral to the formation of a text, but equally essential to its nature is the use of various grammatical cohesive devices, e.g. substitution, ellipsis and conjunction, as explained in Part 2. Orthographic sentences thus contribute written textual information in chunks which together form a unified whole. So, whereas grammatical analysis may be performed over a single sentence, a paragraph or even a whole book, the sentence is more appropriately reinterpreted as a unit of textual structure, and the largest stretch of language carrying grammatical patterns is designated the clause complex.

In the new lexico-grammatical framework reproduced in Figure 8, it will be noticed that Halliday does not include the adjectival group as a separate class of unit.

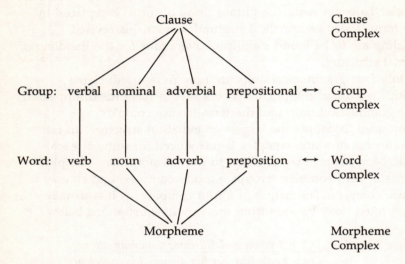

Fig. 8   Revised lexico-grammatical stratum (Halliday:1978:129)

PART 2

SYSTEMIC FUNCTIONAL GRAMMAR

5.   General Nature and Context

5.1 The systemic orientation

In an article on deep grammar, Halliday (1966) lays the
foundations for the enhanced nature of modern systemic
grammar. Here it is mentioned that, for a full grammatical
description, account needs to be taken not merely of the
syntagmatic relations of structure and sequence but also of the
paradigmatic relations of system. Indeed, it is suggested that the
systemic description is the underlying form of representation
since the structural description is derivable from it.

The systemic component, which provides the rationale for the
title of the grammar, derives its name from the fact that it is
made up of systems, each having a set of features which are in
contrast with one another. The properties of a system here are
thus in principle identical to those mentioned in the outline of
scale-and-category syntax (see Section 2.5). However, a major
change of emphasis has occurred in that the category of system
is now accorded such increased prominence that it dominates the
orientation of the grammar.

Each system has as its point of origin a specific rank, and it
may operate either hierarchically:

or simultaneously:

Entry conditions to a point in a system may be either simple:

```
        ┌ xxxxx
  ┌ xxxxx ┤
  │       └ xxxxx
 ─┤       ┌ xxxxx
  └ xxxxx ┤
          └ xxxxx
```

or compound:

```
     ┌ xxxxx
   ┌ ┤
   │ └ xxxxx ) ┌ xxxxx
 { │          ├┤
   │ ┌ xxxxx ) └ xxxxx
   └ ┤
     └ xxxxx
```

A systemic description thus appears as a set of features selected from the range of options drawn from the different networks which together constitute the grammar.

Concurrent with this increased emphasis on the role of the system, systemic grammar formally incorporates a semantic functional dimension. It interprets a language as being an enormous systems network of meaning potential. The task of the grammar is to specify the total grid of options available to a speaker of the language; in other words, it accounts for what the speaker 'can do' linguistically, that is to say, what he 'can mean', and indeed how he can represent the meaning through the lexico-grammar and the phonology. What he actually says or does linguistically is the way he realises or 'actualises' this potential. A grammar displaying the meaning potential which the speaker can utilise and indicating the verbal form which any given meaning takes may properly be described as generative. But the relationship in systemic grammar between meaning potential and actualisation differs sharply from that between competence and performance in transformational grammar. Systemic grammar does not draw any distinction of principle between the meaning potential and the use of that potential in a given context. It does not interpret meaning potential as an idealisation of the knowledge that an educated native speaker has of his language; nor does it see meaning potential as some

43

sort of deep structure, requiring various transformations to produce the surface structures which we actually employ. In systemic grammar the actualisation represents the speaker's selection from the potential: it is a grammar of use.

5.2 Language functions

The incorporation of a semantic functional dimension into the grammar underlines the thesis that language is a social activity taking place in a situational context and that it fulfils a number of social functions. This idea is not new: the work of K. Buhler and of B. Malinowski in the 1930s refers to three such functions: the conative, in which language acts as a form of social control; the expressive, in which language serves to express a speaker's feelings; and the ideational/representational, in which language is a means of communicating ideas. In Halliday's own view, adult language fulfils essentially four main functions: experiential, logical, interpersonal and textual. These will in turn be seen to reflect the different aspects of linguistic meaning.

The experiential function of language is to communicate ideas. It is the function whereby a speaker expresses the content elements of his utterance. In operating this function he refers to people, objects, places, actions, events, states, qualities and circumstances. Thus, for example, the experiential content in the sentence *I bought a new car yesterday* is 'speaker; + action, past — *buy*; + object — *car*, state — *new*; + time — *yesterday*'. In *Your hands are cold* it is 'object, plural — *hand*, possession — addressee; + state, present — *cold*'.

The logical function relates the ideas to each other on an equal or subordinate basis, e.g. *John will be late and Jim can't come at all; He doesn't like raisins but he loves nuts; Although he doesn't like raisins, he loves nuts; If you win this race, you'll be selected for the national team; Kevin, the captain, scores every match; Bill the baker wins every time; Yesterday's treasury announcement, that the inflation rate is falling, is very encouraging; The fact that the inflation rate is falling is very encouraging.*

The interpersonal function of language is firstly to establish and maintain social relations, secondly to influence people's behaviour and 'get things done', and thirdly to express the speaker's feelings, attitudes and opinions. The first of these, the

44

social function, is to be found in greetings and various forms of phatic communion. *Good morning; Hello; Pleased to meet you; Cheerio; Bye* are typical examples of greetings, serving to open, respond to or close social contact. *How are you?; Nice day* are ways of furthering that contact, but they are expressions which could also be used in different circumstances. In the present context, however, *How are you?* is not seeking a comprehensive reply on the state of the interlocutor's health; irrespective of the person's actual condition, it is normal, especially if the participants are not well acquainted, to reply in the vein *Very well, thank you. And you?* or *Not so bad, thank you.* Thus the exchange of utterances in the social function follows very much a formulaic pattern which can be anticipated, and the language used serves merely to open the way for more substantial discourse. Indeed, someone who did break this pattern and embarked on a full account of his ailments in reply to a comparative stranger would quickly be regarded as an oddity. The use of phrases such as *Nice day* or *Lovely weather, isn't it?* in this social function could quite possibly be the prelude to a fairly lengthy conversation about the weather. But, in such circumstances, the conversation is likely to remain on a superficial level because the topic of weather is being used as a subject which can be 'discussed' non-controversially and which can thereby break down the barriers to further communication and interaction.

The second interpersonal function may be termed the instrumental function, which is that of influencing the behaviour of others and getting things done. It manifests itself in a variety of ways, some of which are illustrated below.

request:	*Could you pass the salt, please?*
enquiry:	*What time is the next train to Preston?*
instruction:	*Turn left at the lights and take the first turning right.*
prohibition:	*Keep out; No smoking; Do not lean out of the window.*
warning:	*Danger; Road works; New roundabout ahead.*
advice:	*I would avoid straining your eyes, if I were you.*
threat:	*I'll smack you if you do that again.*

The social and instrumental functions, which are concerned with social and instrumental interaction, are often grouped together as the 'interactional' function, and this term will be used later in the book.

45

The third interpersonal function of language is to express the speaker's own attitudes towards and assessment of the ideational content of what is being said. It is thus referred to as the personal function and serves to moderate the mainstream idea in the sentence, as seen in the following examples:

John has <u>probably</u> arrived by now.
<u>Perhaps</u> she never received the letter.
She <u>may</u> never have received the letter.
He <u>must</u> have arrived by now.
<u>Unfortunately</u> she never received the letter.
<u>Surprisingly</u> he gained a distinction.
<u>Regrettably</u> he has decided to leave.

The textual (or discoursal) function is, according to Halliday, to create texts. It is the function which gives coherence and cohesion to a passage. Consider by way of illustration the following sequence from a children's story from which some of the features of the textual component have been removed.

The boys crept up to the car. The car was parked on the grass verge. The boys peered round the bumper of the car. The boys peered towards the shed. A dim light burned in the shed.

Even this fragment is sufficient to show that any real passage is more than just a succession of sentences. A text makes use of varying types of linguistic resources to link the ideas being expressed and make them hang together. Indeed, without such means the resulting effect is an intolerable passage to read.

Each of the functions is distinct in its own right, but it is emphasised that in most utterances language performs more than one function. Take, for example, the sentence *The porters may have forgotten the keys and gone back for them,* which may be crudely analysed as follows.

experiential:	*The porters have forgotten the keys.*
	The porters have gone back for the keys.
logical:	*and*
interpersonal:	*may*
textual:	deletion in second clause of subject and auxiliary verb *The porters have.*
	deletion in second clause of *may.*
	substitution in second clause of *them* for *the keys.*

The experiential and logical functions together comprise what is termed the ideational function.

The different language functions are accounted for by three components of the grammar, which are named after the functions to which they relate: the ideational component, which has an experiential and a logical sub-component, the interpersonal component and the textual component. The grammar thus has a functional input and a structural output. Although each of the components is discrete, all contribute simultaneously, though in different ways, to the overall meaning and structure of the text. There is no sense of sequential priority accorded to any one particular component. Indeed, Halliday refutes any idea that a speaker first generates the sentence content and then transforms it into the required speech mode and textual sequence.

5.3 Register

Register was described in Section 1.5 as the variety of language used in a particular situational context. The situational context was examined on four parameters: field, tenor, role and mode; and a register was determined by correlating the features of situational context with the lexical, grammatical and phonological features of the text. Situational context was thus viewed as the setting in which linguistic acts take place. More recently, however, it has been suggested that the situational dimensions of register do not merely provide the setting for a text but actually determine its nature.

Register now accounts for the contextual dimensions of social meaning. It represents the socio-contextual or semiotic resources from a socio-cultural system which apply in a given situation, determining the choice of meaning options in the semantic system of the language. The semiotic features of register thus mediate between the social system of a culture and the semantic system of the language. In other words, for any given register a selection of the semiotic features available characterises the situational context and governs the choice of semantic options.

The parameters of register are now grouped under only three headings: field, tenor and mode. Field, which previously specified the subject matter alone, (cookery, physics, sport, politics, religion, etc.), now includes reference to the persons and things involved (persons, things, abstractions, places, events, etc.), to the nature of the activities (actions, events, or states), to the qualities or attributes of the entities involved and to the circumstances of the activities (time, manner, location, etc.).

Tenor is now divided into personal tenor and functional tenor. Personal tenor is concerned with the social roles of participants together with their status relationship and personalities; it thus handles the degrees of formality, familiarity and technicality of linguistic exchanges. In broad terms personal tenor has the responsibility of dealing with the area previously covered by the whole parameter of tenor in the earlier model of register. Functional tenor now embodies the area formerly handled by role; it is concerned with determining the social function or role of an utterance, identifying the purpose for which the language is being used, e.g. description, directions, request, etc.

Mode continues to refer to the medium and channel of the text, as outlined in Section 1.5, and incorporates, as before, various combinations of the basic two modes, spoken and written.

Consequent upon the mediating role which register features now have between the social system and the semantic networks in the linguistic system, the semiotic dimensions of register are directly relatable to the semantic components of the grammar. Field is seen as determining the features of the ideational component, tenor the interpersonal component, and mode the textual component.

5.4 The linguistic system

The inclusion of the semantic level in the grammar makes a considerable difference to the overall appearance of the linguistic system. This is now seen as comprising three layers or strata (in place of the term 'levels'): a semantic stratum, a lexico-grammatical stratum and a phonological stratum. The semantic stratum accounts for the different facets of meaning in a text: ideational, interpersonal and textual. The lexico-grammatical stratum accounts through syntax, morphology and lexis for the wording of the text; it is the level where lexical and grammatical structures which realise the output from the semantic components are mapped onto one another. In short, the lexico-grammatical stratum accounts for the way in which meaning is expressed in words. The phonological stratum accounts through intonation patterning, stress prominence and sound patterning for the sound structure of the text.

Halliday's brief account of the three strata would suggest a simple diagram (Figure 9) to represent the relationship between the three strata and phonetics and register.

	context	register
linguistic system	meaning	semantics
	wording	lexico-grammar
	sound structure	phonology
	sounds	phonetics

Fig. 9   The linguistic system in systemic functional grammar

6. The Ideational Component

The ideational component accounts for the underlying content of an utterance. Under the experiential sub-component it handles all types of processes, qualities, participating entities and circumstances. In this respect, processes include actions, events, states and relations; participating entities (participants) include persons, objects and abstractions; and circumstances involve reference to the time, place, manner, reason, conditions, etc. relating to the process. The relationships between processes and participants are expressed through the transitivity network in this sub-component. In addition, under the logical sub-component are handled the logical relations which exist between the various types and sizes of elements of content; such relations include, for example, coordination, subordination and apposition.

6.1 The experiential sub-component

In the experiential sub-component, transitivity is the area in which there has been most activity. As already stated, transitivity is concerned with types of process and their relationship with the central participants, their attributes and the immediate circumstances. It has as its point of origin the major clause, that is to say a clause containing a predicator. The process is associated with the predicator, the participants with the subject and extensive complement, and attributes with the intensive complement.

In Halliday's writings, two patterns of clause organisation on the dimension of transitivity are outlined: the transitive pattern and the ergative pattern. In the transitive pattern the most prominent participant roles are 'actor', 'goal', 'attributor' and 'attribuant'. Clauses are first characterised according to whether the process is one of action or one of ascription (attribution). Those involving action processes, e.g. *Mary washed the clothes; The recruits marched*, are labelled 'extensive', whereas those concerned with ascription, e.g. *Jill seems happy; John made her happy*, are labelled 'intensive'.

In extensive clauses the verbal action may or may not be directed by the 'actor' towards a 'goal'. A basic distinction is drawn between goal-directed action, labelled 'effective', e.g. *wash, hit, throw,* and non-directed action, known as 'descriptive', e.g. *march, rest, garden, walk.* Another way in which this distinction is expressed is by saying that goal-directed action is inherently associated with two participants, whereas non-directed action is inherently associated with only one participant. In effective clauses, then, the process handles the relationship between actor and goal.

Example:

actor process   goal
Mary washed the clothes.

In descriptive clauses there can also be the possibility of specifying a secondary participant, an 'initiator', discretely from the actor.

Example:

actor   process
The recruits marched.

initiator   process   actor
The sergeant marched the recruits.

The terms 'effective' and 'descriptive' thus form a sub-system of the feature 'extensive'.

Through the system of voice, inherent participant roles are aligned with elements of clause structure. The primary opposition in the voice system is 'middle'/'non-middle'. The choice of 'middle' means that the inherent role(s) associated with the process is(are) realised as a single element of structure, which in English is the subject.

Examples:

effective, middle: *Mary washed* (i.e. washed herself).
descriptive, middle: *The recruits marched.*

In the effective clause the subject embodies the roles of both actor and goal, whereas in the descriptive clause it represents the role of actor alone.

The inherent roles in non-middle clauses are expounded as separate elements. Non-middle clauses select further between 'operative' and 'receptive'. In effective operative clauses the process is directed by the actor as subject onto the goal as complement. The goal may, in fact, be present — 'transitive', or not — 'intransitive'.

Examples:

She washed the clothes.
She washed (i.e. washed the clothes).

In effective receptive clauses the subject realises the function 'goal'.

Example:

The clothes were washed by Mary.

A receptive clause is either 'process-oriented' or 'agent-oriented', and in the latter case the agent may or may not be specified.

Examples:

process-oriented: *These clothes wash well.*

agent-oriented: *These clothes were washed by Mary.*
  These clothes have been washed.

In descriptive operative clauses the action is initiated by the subject and performed by the actor in complement position.

Example:

The sergeant marched the recruits.

This relationship is reversed in receptive clauses, where, as in effective receptives, the initiator may or may not be present.

Example:

The recruits were marched (by the sergeant).

Intensive clauses handle the relationship between 'attributor' (an optional role concerned with the assignment of the attribute), 'attribuant' (the entity to which the attribute is assigned) and 'attribute'. The process is merely one of ascription, and the presence of an attribute in the form of an intensive complement is obligatory and indeed a marker of intensive clauses. In middle voice the process relates the attribuant to the attribute, which may be nominal or adjectival.

Examples:

She is a clever girl.
Jack is a student.
Jill is/seems happy.

Here *she* is classed as *a clever girl* and *Jack* is grouped with those people classed as students, but in *Jill is/seems happy* the complement *happy* is merely a feature which is attributed to *Jill* either directly by the word *is* or remotely by the word *seems*.

In non-middle operative intensive clauses the subject is the attributor responsible for the ascription. The attribuant is expounded by an extensive complement, and the attribute, of course, by an intensive complement.

Examples:

Max considers her a clever girl.
John made her happy.

In intensive receptive clauses the attribuant as subject is related to the attribute through a passive process.

Examples:

She is considered a clever girl (by Max).
She was made happy (by John).

As these last two examples illustrate, the attributor in receptive clauses may be omitted.

The network developed so far may be drawn as in Figure 10.

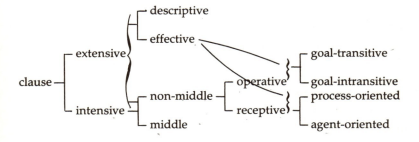

Fig. 10   Transitivity network: transitive pattern

Distinct from goal is the concept of range, the function of which is to specify the scope of the process. The difference between them is not always clear cut, but in general terms the process is not directed towards a range element. Range may represent an entity, abstraction or quantity spanned by or resulting from the process.

Examples:

She sang a song.
He played tennis.
He climbs mountains.
He paid five pounds.
He moved five yards.
He had a bath.
He gave the paint a stir.

Whilst not seeking to diminish the validity of an actor-goal account, Halliday (1968:189) later suggested that an ergative pattern represents a more general form of organisation of transitivity in the clause. The problem with the transitive analysis was that all non-intensive clause types were handled as action clauses, and this is unsuitable to cope with sentences such as *Jim saw the lion; She knows the truth; Everyone liked the play; The play pleased everyone.* The central roles in an ergative pattern are 'causer' and 'affected', and description is concerned with whether the process is caused by a participant other than the one affected by it. An affected participant is thus seen to be common to all clauses apart from those devoid of any participants. Generally speaking, the terms 'causer' and 'affected' replace 'actor' and 'goal' in effective clauses, 'initiator' and 'actor' in descriptive clauses, and 'attributor' and 'attribuant' in intensive clauses. 'Effective' now denotes that the process is inherently associated with the two participants causer and affected, as in *wash*; in other words it marks that the verb is inherently transitive. 'Descriptive' indicates that the process is inherently associated with just one participant, e.g. *march*; that is to say, it is inherently intransitive. A third term, 'nuclear' (later 'neutral') is added for those process types, e.g. *open, stop, train, cook*, etc., which are equally associated with either one or two participants.

Examples:

John opened the door.
The door opened.
The door was opened (by John).

Thus there are now three sub-classes of action process: effective, descriptive and nuclear.

The initial contrast in the voice system remains as before: middle and non-middle. Middle indicates that only one participant, the affected, is actually involved, whilst the non-middle terms 'operative' and 'receptive' mark the involvement of a causer that is distinct from the affected, even if that causer is absent from the actual structure of the clause.

Examples:

middle: *Mary washed* (i.e. washed herself).
            The recruits marched.
            The door opened.

non-middle: *Mary washed the clothes.*
            The sergeant marched the recruits.
            John opened the door.

The terms 'extensive' and 'intensive' disappear in the ergative pattern of organisation, and the whole range of process types is divided into three: 'action' (later 'material'), 'mental' and 'relational' processes. Clauses of relational process may be either equative or attributive.

Examples:

equative: *John is the leader.*
attributive: *John is a good leader.*

In the first of these examples, *John* is equated with — is identified as being — *the leader;* in the second, on the other hand, he is classed among those people who are good leaders. *John,* formerly the attribuant, is the affected participant; *the leader* is equative to the affected participant, whereas *a good leader* is attributive to it. In a non-middle type of relation process clause, the former label 'attributor' is replaced by that of 'causer'.

Example:

John made her happy.

Mental process clauses, e.g. *John saw the lion; She knows the truth; Everyone liked the play,* were not describable appropriately in actor/goal terms, but they can be more satisfactorily accounted for by the concepts of 'processer' and 'phenomenon'.

Examples:

processer   phenomenon
Everyone liked the play.

phenomenon   processer
The play pleased everyone

In ergative terms, *everyone*, the participant whose consciousness is involved, may be labelled the 'affected participant'. The subject *play* in *The play pleased everyone* is then the causer, whereas in *Everyone liked the play* it carries the function of range, denoting the scope of the process. This pair of sentences is thus interpreted as displaying a non-middle/middle contrast.

non-middle: causer   affected
                The play pleased everyone.

middle: affected   range
                Everyone liked the play.

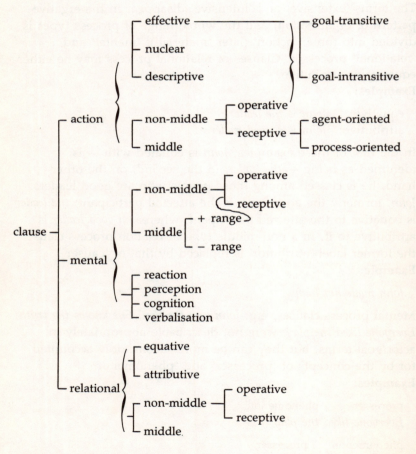

Fig. 11   Transitivity network: ergative pattern

56

Halliday recognises four main sub-types of mental process:

reaction: *He liked the play.*   perception: *He heard a noise.*
cognition: *He believed the story.*   verbalisation: *He said ...*

An abbreviated and slightly modified form of Halliday's network for the ergative pattern of the clause is set out opposite.

Over the years various small modifications have been introduced to both the nature of the network and the nomenclature. For example, the labels 'effective', 'descriptive' and 'nuclear' also appear as 'transitive type', 'intransitive type' and 'neutral'. With this in mind we reproduce overleaf a useful table of Halliday's examples of the network (slightly adapted, from Kress:1976:170).

6.2   The logical sub-component

The logical sub-component is concerned with the various relationships of coordination, subordination and apposition. Two primary types of relationship are identified: paratactic and hypotactic. A paratactic relationship exists between linked elements of equal status.

Examples:

Jack fell down and Jill came tumbling after.
Did Jack fall or was he pushed?
My morning paper, the Daily Guardian, was not delivered today.
Tomorrow, Friday, the eighth of December, is Jean's birthday.

These sentences illustrate relationships of coordination and apposition. In the first pair two alpha clauses are linked, in this instance by the coordinating conjunctions *and* and *or*. In the third sentence the second nominal group, *the Daily Guardian,* is in full apposition to *my morning paper* and could stand on its own as a subject of the sentence. In the fourth example all three elements *tomorrow, Friday* and *the eighth of December* are in apposition.

In a hypotactic relationship one of the elements stands in a subordinate relationship to the other.

Examples:

Before you go, would you sign your names?
If you arrive early, you'll get a better seat.
I love chocolate, which is very bad for me.
John is clever, if stupid.

		non-middle, operative	middle	non-middle, receptive
ACTION PROCESS	transitive type	I can tie the string. | I can tie.	The string tied itself.	The string doesn't tie. | The string wasn't tied (by me).
	neutral type	Mary opened the door. | Mary will open.	The door opened.	This door opens. | The door was opened (by Mary).
	intransitive type	John bounced the ball. |	The ball bounced.	The ball won't bounce. | The ball was bounced (by John).
MENTAL PROCESS	'transitive-like'	The book pleased John. | The book pleases. It doesn't convince you. | It doesn't convince.		John pleases. | John was pleased (by the book). You don't convince. | You aren't convinced (by it).
	'intransitive-like'	John enjoyed the book. You believe it/that ... Mary watched the game. He said nothing/He said that ...	John enjoyed himself. Mary watched. He spoke.	[The book was enjoyed (by John)]. It is believed that ... [The game was watched (by Mary)]. Nothing was said; It was said that ...
RELATIONAL PROCESS	attributive	John made Mary happy. The girls kept the room clean.	Mary was happy. The room kept clean.	Mary was made happy (by John). The room was kept clean (by the girls).
	equative	The chairman was John. A tick represents an acceptance.		John was the chairman. An acceptance is represented by a tick.

In the first two sentences, *before you go* and *if you arrive early* are subordinate to the main clause. In the third example, the non-defining relative clause *which is very bad for me* comments on and is subordinate to the proposition in the main clause. In the fourth sentence, *if stupid* is subordinate to and qualifies the intensive complement *clever*.

Halliday (1977:208 & 210) draws up systems of logical relationships for the clause complex (Figure 12) and the word complex (Figure 13), giving a paradigm chart of types of hypotactic and paratactic occurrence for each.

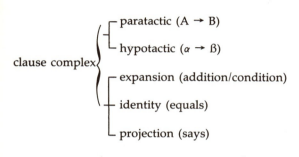

	paratactic	hypotactic
expansion	coordinate	conditional, causal, concessive
identity	appositive	non-defining relative
projection	quoting (direct speech)	reporting (indirect speech)

Fig. 12   Logical sub-component: clause complex

The hypotactic clauses of expansion mentioned here (conditional, causal and concessive) are examples of the type of bound clauses classed as 'conditioning clauses' in Part 1, and the hypotactic identity clauses are bound additioning clauses. Examples of this system of the logical sub-component in relation to the clause complex are given below.

paratactic expansion:
  Jack fell down <u>and Jill came tumbling after</u>.

paratactic identity:
  Jack has everything he could wish for: <u>he enjoys good health, has an interesting job and leads a very varied social life</u>.

paratactic projection:
> *"Have you checked the battery?"*, the mechanic asked.

hypotactic expansion:
> *If you need any help*, give me a call.

hypotactic identity:
> Frank has a new Rolls, *which is amazingly comfortable inside*.
>
> I eat a great deal of chocolate, *which is very bad for me*.

hypotactic projection:
> The mechanic asked *whether we had checked the battery*.

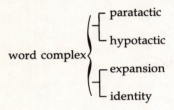

word complex
- paratactic
- hypotactic
- expansion
- identity

	paratactic	hypotactic
expansion	coordinate	modifying
identity	appositive	defining appositive

Fig. 13 Logical sub-component: word complex

(Here the term 'modifying' refers to instances of modification of a headword.) This system, presented above in relation to the word complex, is exemplified below also by reference to the group complex.

paratactic expansion:
> Oranges *and lemons*.

paratactic identity:
> My morning paper, *the Daily Guardian*, was not delivered today.

hypotactic expansion:
> John is clever, *if stupid*.
>
> A *new* broom sweeps clean.

hypotactic identity:
> The fact *that we won* is proof enough.
>
> Jones *the butcher* is moving.

7. The Interpersonal Component

The interpersonal component deals with the interactional and personal aspects of the grammar.

7.1 The interactional sub-component

The interactional sub-component handles the factors pertaining to how a speaker interrelates with others, both socially in establishing channels of communication, and regulatorily and instrumentally in influencing the behaviour of others and in getting things done. For the most part, systemic grammarians have accounted for this area through the system of mood of the clause, as described in Section 2.5.

The system of mood, however, deals only with the syntactic structure of the sentence and not necessarily with what the speaker is doing. Recognising this fact, Fawcett (1980) sets out a system of illocutionary force, which, reflecting the studies on language use undertaken within the branch of linguistics known as pragmatics, covers what may be called the speech function of an utterance. Whilst the labels in Fawcett's illocutionary force system have more in common with the terms 'question', 'command', etc., than 'interrogative', 'imperative', etc., he chooses terms which avoid the need for overlaid explanations of a given speech function. Thus, for example, he does not need to describe *Would you like to go for some bread?* as a question functioning as a request.

Fawcett makes the basic division between utterances dealing with information and those functioning as directives.

Examples:

Ivy'll read it.
Read it.

He distinguishes three main types of information utterances: information giver, e.g. *Ivy'll read it*; information check, e.g. *Ivy'll read it?*; and information seeker, e.g. *Will Ivy read it?*. Directives

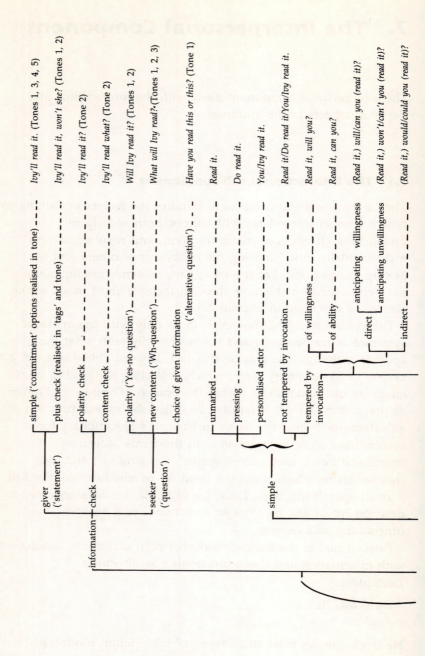

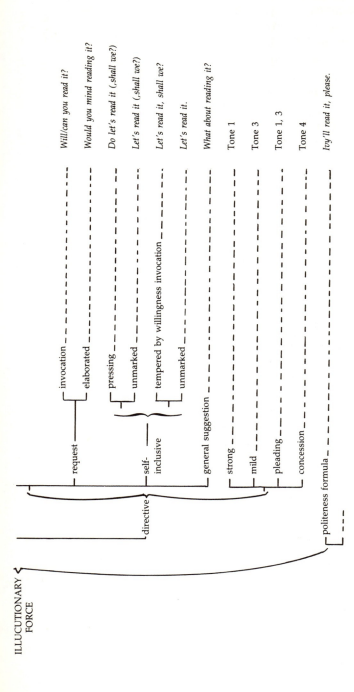

Fig. 14 Illucutionary force (Fawcett:1980:103 slightly adapted)

are classified as simple directives, request directives, self-inclusive directives and general suggestion directives. Simple directives appear most neutrally in the form *Read it*; but they also occur in the more exhortative form *Do read it,* as well as with specific mention of the actor, e.g. *You read it.* Simple directives may also be tempered by invocation, e.g. *Read it, will you/won't you/would you?* Requests typically include invocation in initial position, e.g. *Will you/won't you/would you read it?* Self-inclusive directives are commonly associated with the form *let's* and may also include an invocation, e.g. *Let's read it, shall we?* To complete this sketch of Fawcett's account, Figure 14 on the previous pages shows his system of illocutionary force.

7.2 The personal sub-component

The personal sub-component handles those features relating to the speaker's own contribution to the meaning. The speaker participates by offering, for example, his comment on and reaction towards the main propositional content of the sentence. Illustrations of the speaker's probability assessment of the content are given below.

John has possibly forgotten.
Maybe John has forgotten.
John may have forgotten.
It's possible that John has forgotten.
There's a possibility that John has forgotten.

This particular facet of meaning is accounted for through the system of modality, which handles the scale of probability from possibility to certainty, as illustrated by the following sequence.

It is possible that John has forgotten.
It is probable that John has forgotten.
It is virtually certain that John has forgotten.
It is certain that John has forgotten.

These gradations of probability are drawn up by Halliday (in Kress: 1976) into a system in which the central term 'probable' is first contrasted with the outer terms 'possible' and 'certain' (see Figure 15 opposite).

Halliday (op. cit.) points out that modality elements are expressed by a variety of syntactic forms: verbal, adverbial, adjectival and nominal.

verbs (modal auxiliaries): *may, might, can, could, will, would,*
  should, must, ought to, need.
adverbs: e.g. *maybe, possibly, perhaps, conceivably, probably,*
  presumably, obviously, certainly, definitely, surely.
adjectives: e.g. a) *possible, likely, probable, obvious, certain, definite*
  (in the clause pattern 'It is _____ that ...').
                 b) *sure, certain*
  (in the pattern 'I am _____ that ...').
nouns: e.g. *possibility, chance, likelihood, probability, certainty.*

Fig. 15   Modality (Kress: 1976:194)

It should be pointed out at this juncture that some of the
auxiliary verbs can, of course, also occur with a non-modal
function, contributing instead to the ideational content of the
clause. In such a case they do not form part of the modality
system in the interpersonal component but are handled under
the heading of modulation in the ideational component.
Examples:
  John can come. (is able to)
  You may go now. (are permitted to)
  I must go now. (am obliged to)
Where a clause with a modal element includes a negative, this is
interpreted not as a negative modality but rather as modality
being expressed towards a negative proposition; in other words
the negative element is supplied from the ideational component.
Examples:
  You may not realise that ... = You possibly don't realise that ...
  You won't know that ... = You probably don't know that ...
  You can't believe that ... = You surely don't believe that ...
Reproduced over the page is Halliday's chart of verbal and
adverbial exponents of modality followed by his list of examples.

Modality (interpersonal function)

		Probable	Possible-certain		
			Possible	Virtually certain	Certain
Neutral	POS (i) NEG (i) NEG (ii)	probably will } won't	possibly may, can* (could) may not [can't (couldn't)]		certainly must (will) can't (couldn't) [may not]
Undertone: tentative, deduced	POS (i) NEG (i) NEG (ii)	presumably would (will) } wouldn't (won't)	perhaps might, could might not [couldn't (can't)]	assuredly should, ought to shouldn't, oughtn't to [might not]	obviously must couldn't (can't) [might not]
Overtone: assertive, with reservation (tonic)	POS (i) NEG (i) NEG (ii)	*predictably* (tone 1) *would* } *wouldn't*	*conceivably* (tone 4) *may, might, could* *might not* *[can't, couldn't]*	*surely* (tone 4) *should, ought to* *shouldn't, oughtn't to* *[might not]*	*surely* (tone 1) *must* *can't couldn't* *[may not, might not]*

* normally *may* in declarative, *can* in interrogative

( ) alternative forms

[ ] 'modality negative' forms

(in Kress:1976:191)

positive thesis	negative thesis
Probably this gazebo will be by Wren.	*won't*
Presumably this gazebo would be by Wren.	*wouldn't*
Predictably this gazebo would be by Wren. (falling tone)	*wouldn't*
Possibly this gazebo may be by Wren.	*may not*
Perhaps this gazebo might be by Wren.	*might not*
Conceivably this gazebo might be by Wren. (falling-rising tone)	*might not*
Assuredly this gazebo should/ought to be by Wren.	*shouldn't*
Surely this gazebo should/ought to be by Wren. (falling-rising tone)	*shouldn't*
Certainly this gazebo must be by Wren.	*can't*
Obviously this gazebo must be by Wren.	*couldn't*
Surely this gazebo must be by Wren. (falling tone)	*can't*

(in Kress: 1976:197)

In addition to the speaker's assessment of the probability of the utterance content, the personal sub-component also takes account of the speaker's comment on or attitude towards the utterance content.

Examples:

> *Seriously, I'm horrified.*
> *Understandably, she's sceptical.*
> *Amazingly, he came top.*
> *Luckily, no-one was hurt.*
> *Sensibly, she booked her ticket early.*

This aspect is typically expounded by a particular type of adverbial referred to in Quirk et al. (1972:507-20) as a disjunct. Disjuncts are adverbials which are peripheral to the structure of the clause and which convey the speaker's comment or attitude. Quirk et al. distinguish two types of disjunct: style and attitudinal. Style disjuncts specify the terms in which a person is speaking, whereas attitudinal disjuncts comment on the content of what he is saying. Three classes of style disjunct are listed, relating to

a) the terms of the speaker's mental orientation, e.g. *candidly, frankly, honestly, seriously;*

b) the terms in which the speaker is generalising, e.g. *broadly, crudely, roughly*;

c) other terms of reference, e.g. *literally, metaphorically, personally*.

The scope of Quirk et al.'s attitudinal disjuncts includes the area of probability assessment described under modality. Outside this area, comments on the content of what is being said fall into two main groups: those which are comments on the general content of the clause but not on the action of the subject, and those which comment on the action of the subject as well as on

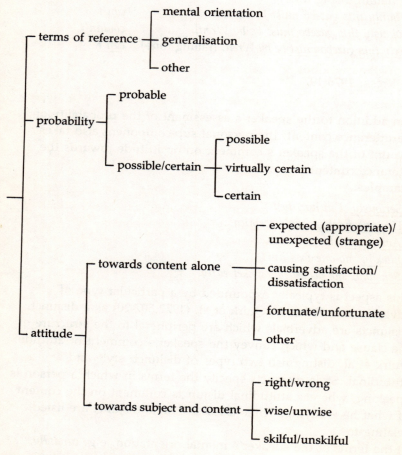

Fig. 16 *Personal sub-component*

the general content. Judgement may be passed that
a) the content
   i) is strange or unexpected, e.g. *amazingly, astonishingly, strangely, remarkably, unexpectedly;*
   ii) is appropriate or expected, e.g. *appropriately, inevitably, naturally, predictably, typically, understandably;*
   iii) causes satisfaction of dissatisfaction, e.g. *annoyingly, disappointingly, regrettably, refreshingly, delightfully;*
   iv) is fortunate or unfortunate, e.g. *fortunately, happily, luckily, sadly;*
   v) (other judgements) e.g. *conveniently, preferably, thankfully.*
b) the subject of the clause and the content
   i) are right or wrong, e.g. *correctly, justly, unjustly, rightly;*
   ii) show wisdom or skill, e.g. *cleverly, foolishly, sensibly, wisely.*

Disjuncts may also be expressed by structures other than single adverbs.

Examples:

in short, to be frank, to my delight,
in all honesty, if I may say so, I'm afraid.

Figure 16, based on the work of both Halliday and Quirk et al., shows a system for the personal sub-component which includes the speaker's terms of reference for the proposition, his probability assessment of it and his attitude towards it.

8. The Textual Component

The textual component accounts for the thematic organisation and the information structure of the propositional content of the sentence. It also handles relationships of cohesion within and between sentences.

8.1 Theme and thematisation

The thematic patterning of a sentence represents the way the elements of the ideational component are organised as a message, in that it is concerned with the sequencing of the elements of clause structure. Thematic structure consists of two basic elements: theme and rheme. That element of the clause which is in first position is known as the theme, and everything that follows it is the rheme.

Examples:

theme	rheme
The results	*will be announced tomorrow.*
Tomorrow	*the results will be announced.*
Announce	*the results tomorrow.*
Have	*you seen the exhibition yet?*
We	*saw the exhibition last Friday.*
The exhibition	*we saw last Friday.*
What	*did you see?*
Frankly	*I'm amazed.*
See	*a Martian we did.*
Did	*you get a newspaper?*
Tired	*you may be.*
John	*they call him.*

The theme is thus the element which the speaker selects as the starting point of his message. It may be realised by the subject, predicator, complement or adjunct, and the above examples are now classified below in terms of the structural element expounding the theme.

| subject: | We saw the exhibition last Friday. |
| | The results will be announced tomorrow. |

predicator:
a) main verb:	Announce the results tomorrow.
	See a Martian we did.
b) auxiliary:	Have you seen the exhibition yet?
	Did you get a newspaper?

| extensive complement: | What did you see? |
| | The exhibition we saw last Friday. |

| intensive complement: | Tired you may be. |
| | John they call him. |

| adjunct: | Tomorrow the results will be announced. |
| | Frankly I'm amazed. |

It is standard practice to distinguish between the 'unmarked' or normal, expected occurrences of the theme element and the 'marked' or less usual forms. Related to the system of mood, this operates in the following way. In a declarative clause the subject as theme is the unmarked form, e.g. *John gave the table to Mary.* In a polar interrogative (anticipating a yes/no answer) the unmarked theme is the finite auxiliary element, e.g. *Did John give*

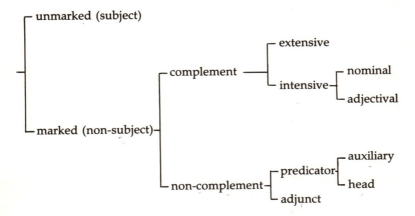

Fig. 17   Theme in the declarative clause

71

the table to Mary? In a WH- interrogative it is the WH- element which is the unmarked theme, e.g. *What did John say to Mary?*; *Where has Bill gone?*, and in an imperative clause it is the imperative form of the verb, e.g. *Give that to me.* Figure 17 on the previous page shows a modification of Halliday's system of theme in declarative clauses, determined by elements of structure and incorporating the concept of markedness.

The theme element may also be interpreted semantically, and in these terms the experiential, logical, interactional and personal sub-components are all represented. (This is the basis of Fawcett's approach.) In a semantic interpretation the theme may be realised typically by an experiential entity as subject.

Examples:

> *John gave Mary the table.*
> *The table was given to Mary.*
> *Mary was given the table.*

Here a distinction may be drawn between the first sentence and the second and third ones. In the first sentence the subject *John* represents the first inherent role associated with the process *give*. In the second and third sentences the subjects *the table* and *Mary* represent the second and third inherent roles. Much less usually the experiential entity may be expounded by an extensive complement (except in a question) or an adjunct.

Examples:

> *The table John gave to Mary.*
> *What did John give Mary?*
> *To Mary John gave the table.*

Still within the experiential sub-component the theme may be provided by part of the process, a circumstance or an attribute.

Examples:

process:
    a) *Give that to me.*
       Go away.
    b) *Did you finish the crossword?*
       Have you heard the news?

circumstance:
    Tomorrow we will give it a test-run.
    Near the lake there was a huge oak tree.
    Where are you going?
    Carefully she undid the wrapping paper.

attribute: *Stupid though you may be ...*
                 Sad am I without thee.

Logical element themes are realised by the type of adverbial referred to by Quirk et al. as conjuncts, which fulfil a connective function between sentences, e.g. *lastly, moreover, similarly, in conclusion, in other words, consequently, otherwise, nevertheless.*

Example:

Nevertheless he is a reliable member.

It should be pointed out, however, that Fawcett is so far the only major systemic grammarian who has handled this area of conjunctive cohesion under the logical sub-component. Halliday regards conjunction as part of the textual component, where in fact he deals with all aspects of grammatical cohesion (see Section 8.3).

From the interpersonal component, interactional theme words are provided by formulaic adjuncts.

Examples:

Please close the door.
Kindly leave the room.

Lastly, theme elements from the personal sub-component may be realised by words from any of the three systems: terms of reference, probability, attitude.

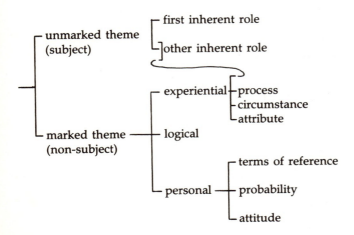

Fig. 18   Theme in the statement (information giver)

Examples:

Briefly, *it's an everlasting paint.*
Perhaps he'll succeed this time.
Wisely Jane ignored him.

Figure 18, on the previous page, which is a modification of Fawcett's schema (1980:161), shows a system of theme in the statement (or rather in the utterance operating as a simple information giver), based on the semantic function of the element in question.

Together with the basic system of 'simple' theme, thematisation takes account of predicated theme and identifying theme. Predicated theme is a facility whereby an entity or circumstance is extracted from the main body of the proposition and expressed in the structural pattern

it + be + _____ + who/that/which ..., which is placed in front of the remainder of the proposition.

Examples:

It was John who told me.
It's the words that Bill knows (not the notes).
It's the glass which is difficult to replace (not the frame).
It was tomorrow that the launch should have taken place.
It was through sheer concentration that he won.

Predicating a theme has the effect of focusing attention on the element circumscribed in this way and thus of highlighting its role in the message. This is the type of structure which in transformational grammar has been called a cleft sentence.

An identifying theme takes one or more elements of the proposition and creates a nominalisation from them, which itself acts as the subject of an intensive clause.

Examples:

What I want is a drink of tea.
What Jill did was (to) prepare the dinner.
What you need is to get away from it all.

Again, in transformational grammar this type of structure is known as a pseudo-cleft sentence.

8.2 Information

The system of information is concerned with how a text is organised into message blocks. Each message block is termed an

74

information unit and is composed of the structural elements
'given' and 'new'.

Examples:

| new   new |
| [*What's happening tomorrow?*] |*We're climbing Ben Nevis.*| |

| new   given   new |
| [*What are we doing tomorrow?*] |*We're*| *climbing Ben Nevis.*| |

| new   given   new |
| [*What are we climbing tomorrow?*] |*We're climbing*|*Ben Nevis.*| |

Thus in the first example the whole of the reply *We're climbing
Ben Nevis* is analysed as a new element in the context of the
preceding question. In the second example the question is such
that only the predicator and complement in the reply are new.
The reply in the third example contains still more information
which has already appeared in the question, as a result of which
only the complement *Ben Nevis* constitutes additional, new
information.

The use of the terms 'given' and 'new' does not necessarily
mean that the elements have or have not been previously
mentioned. Rather, a given element is one which is presented by
the speaker as recoverable (by the hearer) from previous
discourse, whereas a new element is one which is regarded by
the speaker as not being recoverable. In any particular situation
it is quite possible for the position presented by a speaker not to
correlate with reality; typically he may, by using a pronoun, treat
an element as given and therefore recoverable when in the
interpretation by the listener it is not.

It is through this given/new structure that information units in
a text are related to each other and a coherent message is
developed. Of course, although an information unit is processed
in terms of a given/new structure, it is only the new element
which is obligatory: the given element is optional. In other
words, in order for a stretch of language to be a unit of
information at all, it must contain an element of new
information. Commonly, though by no means always, an
information unit extends over a whole clause.

Information units are realised phonologically as tone groups,
one tone group representing one information unit. Each tone
group has a peak of prominence known as the tonic, and it is

this tonic prominence, generally perceived as stress, which marks the place where the focus of attention in the new information occurs. Each information unit thus has an information focus. This normally falls on the final lexical item, and in such instances it is referred to as unmarked. Where it occurs on a non-final item, it is said to be marked.

Examples:

unmarked focus:
> [*Where have you been?*] *We've been to Edinburgh.*
> [*What did you get?*] *I bought some rock.*

marked focus:
> [*Who mowed the lawn?*] *I did.*
> [*What did you do to the lawn?*] *I just mowed it.*
> [*Where have you weeded today?*] *I did the front garden.*
> [*Have you made any progress with the painting?*] *I've given the lounge a first coat.*

8.3 Cohesion

Cohesion is a relationship between elements of a text where proper interpretation and understanding of one element depends on another. It thus serves to relate elements of a text to each other. Grammatical cohesion is achieved through a number of devices: reference and substitution, ellipsis, and conjunction.

8.3.1 Reference and substitution

Reference is seen as the meaning relationship which links full lexical expression of an entity or circumstance with the pro-form/substitute which refers to it. Substitution, on the other hand, is a formal relationship; it is the 'structural mechanism', as Halliday puts it, for signalling the connection between the full lexical expression and the pro-form/substitute. Reference is thus a semantic relationship, whereas substitution is lexico-grammatical.

The various markers refer either back to something that has already been mentioned (or implied), in which case they have anaphoric reference, or forward to something which is about to be said, in which case they have cataphoric reference. Anaphoric and cataphoric reference, in referring to other elements within the text, are both instances of endophoric reference.

Examples:

anaphoric:

> *All this year's students passed. It was very gratifying.*
> *Jill washed the clothes and then ironed them.*

cataphoric:

> *This is the quickest route. Turn left at the lights, straight on to a*
> *roundabout, then right ...*
> *It's the most scenic way, my route.*

Contrasting with endophoric reference is exophoric reference. This involves the use of a pro-form which refers not to another element in the text but rather to an element which is derivable solely from the situation.

Examples: (presupposing no previous mention)

> *It's worked.*
> *Have you finished that book yet?*
> *Did you see that?*
> *She's a bonnie lass.*

Exophoric reference is thus not a textual relation but a situational one; it is therefore not pursued further here.

Anaphoric reference — reference back to something which has already been stated — makes use of substitute pro-forms and other markers to establish identity with the lexical element(s) in question. They may refer back to a variety of different sizes and types of element. (The actual class of the referential form depends, of course, on the function it has in its own clause.)

clause:

> *Everyone has passed. It's amazing.*
> *Jill will have a successful career. I'm sure of that.*
> *Ben has decided to move. Jack told me so.*

predicator ± complement/adjunct:

> *Jill collects stamps now, and she enjoys it.*
> *Rovers will be relegated, and so will City.*
> *Last week I cycled to work, and Mary did the same.*

nominal group:

> *Frank is a good student academically, and he is in the college athletics*
> *team.*

77

Ted bought a new watch and then lost it.
That's a smart bike. I've only got an old one.
A decent dictionary, that's what you need.
Ted has lost his watch.

adjunct:

I shall be seeing Bill tomorrow evening and will tell him then about our plans.
We went to the Isle of Skye this summer. Have you ever been there?
John looks after his car with the utmost care and attention. I wish he treated his clothes like that.

Cataphoric reference involves reference forward to something which is going to be specified more fully. It tends to be confined to relationships between the pro-form and forthcoming clauses or nominal groups.

Examples:

I don't believe it. Jim's actually got a job.
This'll be your best plan. Ring the office first thing tomorrow and ask...
It's easy, this translation.
That was a pleasant surprise, your promotion.

8.3.2 Ellipsis

Ellipsis is the term applied to denote the lack of repetition of one or more elements which have been mentioned in a previous part of the discourse; reference to them is implied and expected to be understood without further mention of them. Ellipted elements are thus deemed to be recoverable by the hearer from the preceding linguistic context. A wide range of elements can be ellipted, and some of the main types are illustrated below.

clause:

Jill has gone abroad. Does Ken know _____ ?
Max is in hospital. Ben told me _____ .
Will you help me fix this shelf, please? Certainly _____ .
Jill has gone abroad. Why _____ ?

predicator + complement:

She was only watching the match because you were _____ .
John accepted the proposal when you did _____ .
The school will buy a computer if the authority won't _____ .
Has Frank paid the bill yet? Yes, he has _____ .

subject + predicator:
Did you see the king? No, _____ the queen.
Has Ben sold his car? No, _____ his bike.
Does Bill live in Glasgow? No, _____ in Edinburgh.

subject + predicator (auxiliary):
John has gone abroad. _____ Gone abroad?
Have you lost your key? No, _____ just left it at home.

predicator:
John *lost* his wallet and Bill _____ his passport.
Dave *has brought* a mower and Ken _____ some shears.

predicator (−auxiliary):
Jack has *agreed* but Tony hasn't _____ yet.
Jill can *come* but Frank won't _____.

subject:
Jack fell down and _____ broke his crown.
Jill tripped and _____ lost her footing.
What did *you* do when you saw what had happened?
_____ Rang the police, of course.

intensive complement:
We were *very annoyed*. Weren't you _____?
Mummy, Mandy is *ill*. Will I be _____?

adjunct:
Frank was *in hospital* when you were _____.
Geoff will go *to the concert* if you'll come _____.
Yesterday I cleaned the window-frames and _____ Jim painted them.

In avoiding full or even partial repetition of an element, the use of ellipsis and anaphoric pro-forms reduces the overall amount of information to be scanned by the recipient. Furthermore, as repeated reference to an element is normally interpretable as part of the given information, these devices obviate the inclusion of lexical strings which do not contribute to the new information content; in this way they reduce the degree of redundancy in the message.

8.3.3   Conjunction

Conjunctive cohesion serves to relate sentences to each other in various types of logical relation. Indeed, Fawcett (1980:178) includes types of conjunction as another aspect of the logical component which he calls 'supplementary linkage', alongside paratactic and hypotactic relations. Halliday (1976:226-73) handles conjunctive adjuncts under four main headings: additive, adversative, causal and temporal.

Additive conjunction serves to further the discourse topic. It differs from the paratactic relation of coordination by introducing the new clause as an extra piece of information, perhaps reinforcing what has already been said.

Compare:

The party got to the summit and had their lunch. And they had time for a rest afterwards.

Here the first *and* coordinates the propositions *the party got to the summit* and *had their lunch*. The second *and*, however, introduces a supplementary idea. Adversative conjunction is explained as introducing an item of information which is 'contrary to expectation'.

Example:

He worked very hard. Yet he didn't pass.

Causal conjunction marks the relationships of reason, consequence and purpose.

Example:

He didn't pass this time, so he will have to resit.

Temporal conjunction specifies the time sequence relationship which exists between sentences.

Examples:

First he forgot his money, then he forgot his keys.
Previously he had never been absent for a day.

Within each of the four broad headings Halliday itemises a range of sub-classes. A selection of these is given below together with examples of the adverbial, prepositional and other expressions which expound them.

additive

additive: *and, also, furthermore, in addition, besides, moreover, incidentally.*
alternative: *or, or else, alternatively.*
expositive/exemplificatory: *that is (to say), in other words, for instance, for example.*
similarity: *likewise, similarly, in the same way.*
contrastive: *by contrast, conversely, on the other hand.*

adversative

adversative: *yet, but, though, however, nevertheless.*
avowal: *in fact, actually, as a matter of fact, really.*
replacive/corrective: *instead, rather, at least, I mean.*
dismissive: *anyhow, at any rate, in any case.*

causal

reason/consequence: *for this reason, because of this, accordingly, on this basis, so, thus, therefore, consequently, as a result.*
purpose: *for this purpose, with this in mind, to this end.*
condition/circumstance: *then, in that case, under the circumstances.*
focus: *in this respect, with regard to this, in this connection.*

temporal

temporal: *previously, up to now, hitherto, at the same time, from now on, henceforward.*
enumerative: *first, next, secondly, then, to begin with, finally.*
summative: *to sum up, in all, in a word, in short.*

Selected Bibliography

This bibliography is a list of the principal books and articles on systemic grammar; it is certainly not exhaustive. For students interested in pursuing areas covered by the book, the following references are suggested for initial reading:

syntax, scale-and-category grammar: Berry (1975, 1977), Muir (1972), Scott et al. (1968), Young (1980);

semantics, functional grammar: Halliday (1970b, 1972, 1977, forthcoming), Kress (1976), Fawcett (1980);

context: Gregory & Carroll (1978), Halliday (1978).

Berry, M. (1975) *Introduction to systemic linguistics: 1, structures and systems*. London: Batsford.

Berry, M. (1977) *Introduction to systemic linguistics: 2, levels and links*. London: Batsford.

Butler, C.S. (1979) 'Recent work in systemic linguistics'. *Language teaching and linguistics: abstracts*, 12.1. Cambridge: Cambridge University Press.

Fawcett, R.P. (1974-76/1981) *Some proposals for systemic syntax: an iconoclastic approach to scale and category grammar*. Polytechnic of Wales: Department of Behavioural and Communication Studies.

Fawcett, R.P. (1980) *Cognitive linguistics and social interaction: towards an integrated model of a systemic functional grammar and the other components of a communicating mind*. Heidelberg: Julius Groos, and Exeter University.

Gregory, M. and Carroll, S. (1978) *Language and situation: language varieties and their social contexts*. London: Routledge & Kegan Paul.

Halliday, M.A.K. (1961) 'Categories of the theory of grammar'. *Word*, 17, 241-92.

Halliday, M.A.K. (1963) 'Class in relation to the axes of chain and choice in language'. *Linguistics*, 2, 5-15.

Halliday, M.A.K., McIntosh, A. and Strevens, P. (1964) *The linguistic sciences and language teaching*. London: Longman.

Halliday, M.A.K. (1966) 'Some notes on "deep" grammar'. *Journal of Linguistics*, 2, 57-67.

Halliday, M.A.K. (1967-8) 'Notes on transitivity and theme in English', 'Parts 1-3'. *Journal of Linguistics*, 3, 37-81 & 199-244 and 4, 179-215.

Halliday, M.A.K. (1970a) 'Functional diversity in language'. *Foundations of Language*, 6, 332-61.

Halliday, M.A.K. (1970b) 'Language structure and language function' in Lyons, J. (ed.) *New horizons in linguistics*. Harmondsworth: Penguin.

Halliday, M.A.K. (1972) 'Options and functions in the English clause' in Householder, F.W. (ed.) *Syntactic theory 1: structuralist*. Harmondsworth: Penguin.

Halliday, M.A.K. (1973) *Explorations in the functions of language*. London: Edward Arnold.

Halliday, M.A.K. and Hasan, R. (1976) *Cohesion in English*. London: Longman.

Halliday, M.A.K. (1977) 'Text as semantic choice in social contexts' in van Dijk, T.A. and Petöfi, J.S. (eds.) *Grammars and descriptions*. Berlin: de Gruyter.

Halliday, M.A.K. (1978) *Language as social semiotic*. London: Edward Arnold.

Halliday, M.A.K. (1979) 'Modes of meaning and modes of expression: types of grammatical structure and their determination by different semantic functions' in Allerton, D.J., Carney, E. and Holdcroft, D. (eds.) *Function and context in linguistic analysis*. Cambridge: Cambridge University Press.

Halliday, M.A.K. and Martin, J.R. (eds.) (1981) *Readings in systemic linguistics*. London: Edward Arnold.

Halliday, M.A.K. (forthcoming) *An introduction to functional grammar*. London: Edward Arnold.

Huddleston, R.D. (1965) 'Rank and depth'. *Language*, 41, 574-86.

Huddleston, R.D. (1981) 'A fragment of a systemic description of English' in Halliday, M.A.K. and Martin, J.R.

Hudson, R.A. (1967) 'Constituency in a systemic description of the English clause'. *Lingua*, 18, 225-50.

Hudson, R.A. (1971) *English complex sentences: an introduction to systemic grammar*. Amsterdam: North Holland.

Hudson, R.A. (1974) 'Systemic generative grammar'. *Linguistics*, 139, 5-42.

Joos, M. (1962) *The five clocks*. The Hague, Mouton.

Kress, G. (ed.) (1976) *Halliday: system and function in language*. London: Oxford University Press.

Leech, G.N. (1966) *English in advertising*. London: Longman.

McIntosh, A. and Halliday, M.A.K. (1966) *Patterns of language: papers in general, descriptive and applied linguistics*. London: Longman.

Muir, J. (1972) *A modern approach to English grammar: an introduction to systemic grammar*. London: Batsford.

Quirk, R., Greenbaum, S., Leech, G. and Svartvik, J. (1972) *A grammar of contemporary English*. London: Longman.

Scott, F.S., Bowley, C.C., Brockett, C.S., Brown, J.G. and Goddard, P.R. (1968) *English grammar: a linguistic study of its classes and structures*. London: Heinemann.

Sinclair, J. McH. (1972) *A course in spoken English: grammar*. London: Oxford University Press.

Young, D.J. (1980) *The structure of English clauses*. London: Hutchinson.

Index

Numbers in bold type mark places where an entry is the heading of a section or sub-section of the book.

contextual function, 14-15
co-ordinating conjunction, 26, 57, 59
copular verb, 28

δ, *see* delta
d, *see* deictic and determiner
declarative mood, 15, 17, 19-20
deictic, 26-27
delicacy, **24-29**
delta, 24, 29
depth, **29-30,** 31-33
descriptive process, 51-52, 54, 56
determiner, 26-28
directive, 61-64
discontinuity, **34-35**
discoursal function, 46
discourse, 5-6, 78
disjunct, 67-69
disjunctive interrogative, 19-20
double function nominals, 10-11

ε, *see* epsilon
effective process, 51-52, 54, 56
element of structure, 9, 10, 12, 23, 29, 31, 34
ellipsis, 39, 76, **78-79**
embedded recursion, 31, 33
endophoric reference, 76-78
entry condition, 17, 43
epsilon, 24
equative clause, 21, 25, 55-56, 58
ergative pattern, 50, 54, 56
exclamation, 14
exclamative mood, 14, 19-20
exophoric reference, 77-78
expansion, 59-60
experiential function, 44-47
experiential sub-component, **50-57,** 72
exponence, **23-24**
extensive clause, 22-23, 50-52

extensive complement, 20-23, 25, 50, 53, 71-72

field, 5, 47-48
finiteness, 18
focus, 74, 76
foot, 3-4
form, **2,** 3, 6, 39
formality, degree of _____, 6, 48
free clause, 15, 17, 24-25
functional tenor, 48
functions of language, **44-47**

γ, *see* gamma
gamma, 24, 30
given information, 75
goal, 50-55
goal-transitive/intransitive, 53, 56
grammar, 2, 6, 43
grammatical pattern, 7-8
graphology, 3-4
group, 7, 9, 12, 16, 26-29
group complex, 39-40, 60
group structure, 12, 18, 26-29, 33

h, *see* headword
headword, 12, 16, 23, 26-29, 60, 71
hypotactic recursion/relationship, 31-33, 57, 59-60, 80

ideational component, 48, **50-60,** 70
ideational function, 44-47
identifying theme, 74
identity, 59-60
illocutionary force, 61-64
imperative mood, 15, 17, 19-20, 61, 72

86

indicative mood, 15, 17, 19-20
information, **74-76,** 80
information giver/
    check/seeker, 61-64, 73-74
inherent role, 51, 54, 72-73
initiator, 51-52, 54
instrumental function, 45-47
intensive clause, 22-23, 50,
    52-53, 74
intensive complement, 20-23,
    25, 50, 52-53, 59, 71, 79
interactional function, 45
interactional sub-component,
    61-64, 72
interlevel, 3, 5, 6
interpersonal component,
    48, **61-69,** 73
interpersonal function, 44-47, 66
interrogative mood, 15, 17, 61
intonation, 4, 49

jussive imperative, 19-20

language functions, **44-47**
levels of language, **2-6**
    see also linguistic system
lexical element, 29
lexical item, 3, 23
lexical set, 3
lexical verb, 22, 29
lexico-grammar, 39-40, 48-49, 76
lexis, 2, 6
limiter, 27
linear recursion, 31-33
linguistic strata/system, **48-49**
    see also levels of language
logical function, 44, 46-47
logical sub-component, 47, 50,
    57-60, 72

m, see modifier
main verb, 36
major clause, 14-15, 18, 50

marked theme, 71-73
meaning potential, 43
medium, see mode
mental process, 55-56, 58
message/message block, 70,
    74-75, 79
middle clause, 18, 51-52,
    54-56, 58
minor clause, 14-15
modality, 64, 66, 68
mode, 5, 47-48
modifier, 12, 23, 26-28, 60
mood, 14, 61
mood system, 19-20, 71
morpheme, 7-9, 39
morpheme complex, 39-40
morphology, 2, 48

negative modality, 65-67
new information, 75, 79
node, 29, 30
nominal group, 10-12, 16, 26-29,
    36-37, 39, 52, 57, 64, 71, 77-78
non-jussive imperative, 19-20
non-middle clause, 51-56, 58
non-polar interrogative, 19
notational symbols, 7, 19, 33
    34
nuclear process, 54, 56
number, 18

object, 20
operative clause, 52-53, 55-56, 58
optative imperative, 19-20

p, see particle and preposition
P, see predicator
paratactic
recursion/relationship, 31-33,
    57, 59-60, 80
participant, 3, 6, 50-51, 54-56
participant role, 50-52, 54
particle, 28

subject, 10-11, 15-16, 21, 23, 36,
  39, 46, 50-51, 53, 70-73, 79
subordinating conjunction, 26
  57
substance, **2,** 3, 6
substitution, 46, **76-78**
syllable, 3, 4
syntax, 2, 31-32, 48, 61, 64
system, **16-23,** 25, 42-44, 53,
  56, 59, 60, 62-63
systemic orientation, **42-44**

temperer, 27
temporal conjunction, 80-81
tenor, 5-6, 47-48
tense, 18
term in system, 16-17
text, 2, 39, 75-77
textual component, 48, **70-81**
textual function, 46
theme, **70-74**
tone group, 3, 4, 75
tonic, 75
transitive pattern, 50-53
transitivity, 19, 20-23,
  50-57
transitivity system, 19-20, 22,
  25, 53, 56

unit, **7-8,** 10, 16, 23, 31,
  33, 40, 75
unmarked theme, 71-73

verb, 28-29, 36-37, 71,
verbal group, 10, 13, 16,
  28-29, 35, 64-65
verbalisation process, 56-57
voice, 18, 51, 54
volitive imperative, 19-20
word, 7, 9, 23, 39
word complex, 39-40, 59-60
word structure, 13

Z-element, 10, 16, 23, 36